The Flourishing Entrepreneurial Lifestyle

Habits and Principles for Personal Growth, Business Success, and Building Your Dream Life

Aiman Kabli

AUTHORITY
PUBLISHING

1st Edition 2025.

ISBN (Paperback): 978-1-965480-07-6

ISBN (eBook): 978-1-965480-08-3

Authority Publishing

www.authority-publishing.com

Printed in the United States of America.

Contents

Preface

Entrepreneurship is a journey that challenges every aspect of who we are. Beyond the late nights of brainstorming, the pursuit of growth, and the risks we take, lies the deeper realization: success is not just about building thriving businesses—it's about creating lives where we, as entrepreneurs, also thrive.

Over the years, I've traveled to over 95 countries, launched startups, mentored hundreds of founders, and collaborated with visionary investors through platforms like *eleva8or*. Along this journey, I noticed something remarkable: the most successful entrepreneurs were not simply surviving but thriving. They cultivated lifestyles that nurtured their physical, mental, and spiritual growth, enabling them to innovate, adapt, and lead purposefully.

I call this way of life the *Flourishing Entrepreneurial Lifestyle (FELS)*—a holistic framework that aligns entrepreneurial ambition with personal fulfillment. Grounded in ten interconnected pillars, FELS offers a roadmap for thriving not just in your work but in every dimension of life, from creativity and continuous learning to physical health and spiritual depth.

This book is my effort to share what I've learned about building a life that complements entrepreneurial ambition. It is a guide to aligning purpose with performance and principles with profit to approach your work and life with balance, clarity, and fulfillment.

Whether you're an aspiring entrepreneur looking to build your first venture or a seasoned founder seeking deeper meaning in your journey, this book offers the tools to flourish in business and every aspect of life. Because entrepreneurship isn't just about solving problems for others; it's about building a life you truly want to live.

Entrepreneurship is a journey like no other—an exhilarating blend of ambition, creativity, and relentless pursuit of growth. Yet, it is also fraught with challenges that test our skills, resilience, balance, and vision. Many embark on this journey with a singular focus on their ventures, only to discover that true success lies in something far greater: flourishing as individuals while building impactful enterprises.

This realization came to me after years of immersion in the entrepreneurial world. Having traveled to over 95 countries, founded multiple startups, and mentored hundreds of entrepreneurs globally, I've had the privilege of observing what sets thriving entrepreneurs apart. These are not just individuals who excel at technical skills or strategy; they embody a holistic lifestyle that fuels their ability to innovate, adapt, and lead purposefully.

I've also had the opportunity to collaborate with and learn from some of the world's most accomplished entrepreneurs and investors. From sharing stages at global conferences to engaging in candid, behind-the-scenes conversations, these experiences have deepened my understanding of what it takes to flourish in the ever-evolving landscape of entrepreneurship. These lessons are not mine alone—they come from a collective wealth of knowledge shared by visionary leaders who have generously contributed their insights to this book.

The Flourishing Entrepreneurial Lifestyle (FELS) is the culmination of these learnings. It introduces a framework that goes beyond conventional business advice, focusing instead on the ten pillars of a lifestyle designed to nurture every aspect of an entrepreneur's growth. These pillars—from creativity and continuous learning to spirituality and health—are not abstract ideals but actionable principles that I've seen transform lives and businesses.

This book is also enriched by the perspectives of world-class entrepreneurs who embody these principles. Throughout its chapters, you'll find stories, reflections, and advice from in-depth interviews with these remarkable individuals. Their experiences testify to the power of adopting a flourishing mindset, showing how it has helped them navigate challenges, innovate solutions, and leave a lasting impact on their communities and industries.

Whether at the beginning of your entrepreneurial journey or seeking to elevate your current path, this book offers a roadmap to align your ambitions with a life well-lived. It is not just about building successful ventures—it's about cultivating the resilience, creativity, and balance to thrive in every dimension of your life.

I invite you to explore FELS's principles, embrace its philosophy, and join a global community of entrepreneurs committed to creating meaningful change. Together, let us redefine what it means to succeed—not as a destination but as a way of life.

Introduction

Flourishing in the Complexity of Entrepreneurship

ENTREPRENEURSHIP IS OFTEN PORTRAYED as a relentless pursuit—a test of ambition, perseverance, and grit. But success in this demanding journey requires more than technical expertise or hard work. The most thriving entrepreneurs don't just excel professionally; they flourish holistically, nurturing every aspect of their lives.

This book introduces the *Flourishing Entrepreneurial Lifestyle (FELS)*—a framework designed to transform how entrepreneurs approach their journey. Rooted in holistic principles, FELS emphasizes the importance of nurturing the mind, body, and spirit alongside mastering the hard skills of running a business. It's a lifestyle that prepares you to thrive in every dimension, helping you weather challenges and seize opportunities with clarity and confidence.

Why FELS Matters

Over the years, I've had the privilege of wearing many hats: industrial engineer, corporate leader, entrepreneur, mentor, and lifelong learner. My career has spanned roles with renowned organizations like *Unilever*, *Emirates* Airlines, and the *International Monetary Fund*. But in my journey as a serial entrepreneur—founding and investing in technology startups, including platforms like *eleva8or.com*—I discovered entrepreneurship's true complexity.

Beyond the boardrooms and business plans, I found fulfillment in mentoring hundreds of startups and ecosystem entities worldwide. From judging competitions to delivering talks at incubators and accelerators, these experiences revealed a universal truth: success comes not just from technical prowess but from a balanced, flourishing lifestyle.

My life outside of work has been just as dynamic. I've lived in multiple countries, including the U.S., UAE, and Saudi Arabia, and visited over 86 nations. Along the way, my interests in health, science, photography, and the arts have fueled my curiosity and creativity—qualities that have proven invaluable in my entrepreneurial pursuits.

These diverse experiences have shaped the FELS philosophy you'll explore in this book. It's a culmination of lessons learned from my own journey and enriched by the insights of world-class entrepreneurs who have shared their stories and strategies.

The 10 Pillars of the Flourishing Entrepreneurial Lifestyle

At the heart of FELS are ten foundational pillars, each addressing a vital component of an entrepreneur's growth and well-being. These pillars provide a roadmap to creating a balanced, purpose-driven life. I have spent many years aspiring to grow in all these areas and help spread awareness of them to others.

Note: the list is in random order and doesn't signify relative priority.

Ideation and Creation

A passion for ideation and creation, i.e., coming up with new ideas for addressing market problems and improving quality of life, formulating proper solutions and models with a solid foundation of business acumen and some common sense and "street smarts."

Self-Discovery & Improvement

A strong drive for self-discovery and improvement, emotional intelligence, and strength of character. Also, having a good sense for discovering and polishing the talents of others, putting the right talents in the right places to unlock maximum potential.

Continuous Learning

Continuously adding and updating knowledge through study, reading, curiosity, and inquisitive conversation. This goes with a drive for thought leadership and a love for sharing knowledge through teaching or mentorship.

Following Technology Trends

Being on the leading edge of technology—following the latest innovations and scientific developments with a focus on deep fields that stretch the limits of human capability.

Travel & Exploration

A love of travel and exploration, understanding different cultures and motivations, embodying the global citizen and digital nomad lifestyle.

Using the Right Tools

Finding and using the right tools (products, devices, hacks, software, etc.) for the right purpose.

Healthy Lifestyle Habits

Healthy lifestyle habits that support mental clarity and performance, such as healthy eating, physical fitness, and good sleep.

Strong Spiritual Depth

Strong spiritual depth and practice (per one's faith) and a drive to serve one's nation and society.

Open & Balanced Mindset

An open mindset that is attracted to novelty, sound logic, good ethics, balance, and elegance, rejecting biases, intolerance, and bickering.

Diverse Hobbies & Activities

Having diverse hobbies and activities that challenge the mind to stretch further and reach greater heights, such as learning languages or appreciating arts and creative pursuits.
Finding beauty and fun in everything we do!

This formula can help us improve at complex entrepreneurship pursuits, challenging business undertakings, or any career aspirations by making us the best versions of ourselves mentally and physically. From what I have seen in the people who embody it, this lifestyle can benefit its followers, starting with substantial income and influential status in society, making lifelong dreams and ambitions come true, and having a fulfilling life full of excitement and adventure! It also aims, of course, to improve the whole world around us and help make it a better place for everyone.

To help spread awareness about this, I recently started a global content movement to share and publish useful lifestyle insights in a specialized blog (https://myfels.com/posts/) and numerous regionally-targeted social media channels, currently posting in 14 languages (a collection of these posts is available at the back of this book). I have also dedicated my website (https://aimankabli.com/) to this cause, using examples from my life and ongoing journey to demonstrate these pillars in action.

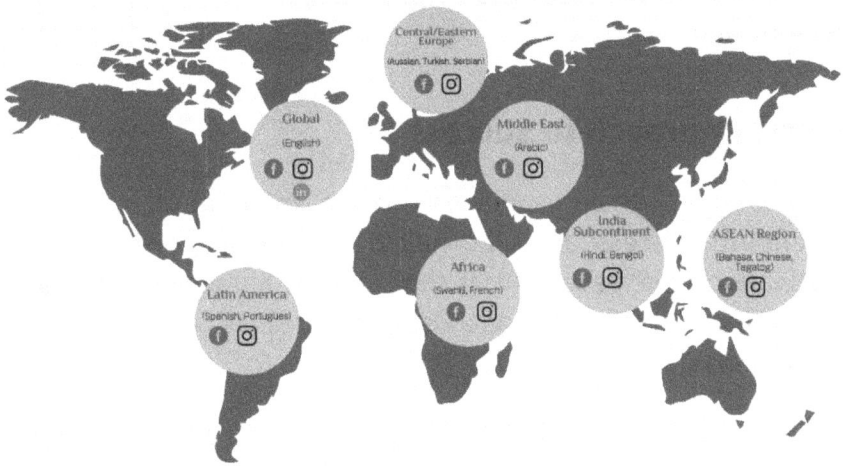

What You'll Find in This Book

I wrote this book as a simplified and practical guide to embracing these principles in the best possible way. This book is divided into three parts:

1. **The Philosophy of FELS**: An exploration of the origins and principles of the FELS framework, including my personal journey and insights from global entrepreneurs.

2. **The 10 Pillars in Action:** This book includes chapters dedicated to each pillar, offering practical examples, real-world strategies, and actionable advice.

3. **Stories of Flourishing Entrepreneurs**: This section features interviews and case studies that showcase how world-class entrepreneurs have embraced the FELS lifestyle and transformed their personal and professional lives.

This book is enriched by insights from interviews with world-class entrepreneurs who have successfully embodied the principles of FELS. Their stories offer actionable strategies and inspiration, showcasing how these pillars can transform your ventures and personal life.

A New Approach to Success

FELS is not just a framework—it's a movement. It's about redefining success as a journey of flourishing rather than a destination of achievement. It challenges the traditional narrative of entrepreneurship, offering a vision of a lifestyle that is as fulfilling as it is impactful.

As you read this book, I invite you to reflect on your journey and consider how these principles can enrich your life. By embracing the FELS mindset, you're not just preparing to succeed in business but crafting a life that inspires and sustains you, even in the face of uncertainty.

Through this journey, I hope to guide you toward a new perspective on entrepreneurship that helps you build successful ventures and inspires you to thrive holistically. Let's redefine what it means to flourish as entrepreneurs and individuals.

This is your opportunity to flourish. Let's begin.

Pillar 1: Ideation and Creation

IDEAS ARE THE FOUNDATION of every great entrepreneurial journey. They spark innovation, solve problems, and fuel progress. But ideation isn't just about having an "aha" moment—it's about fostering a mindset that consistently generates valuable and actionable ideas. This chapter explores the first pillar of the *Flourishing Entrepreneurial Lifestyle (FELS)*: *Ideation and Creation*. We'll uncover how successful entrepreneurs harness the power of creativity to transform challenges into opportunities and build solutions that resonate with their audience.

Through real-world examples and actionable insights, you'll discover how to cultivate an idea-driven mindset and leverage creativity to unlock opportunities, generate multiple income streams, and create meaningful impact.

What It's All About

At its core, "Ideation and Creation" is about seeing possibilities where others see obstacles. Whether it's revolutionizing an industry or addressing unmet needs, the ability to generate ideas and execute them effectively defines successful entrepreneurs.

The main aim is to identify potential needs and formulate proper solutions and models for them to generate value and improve the world around us. This is aided by a solid foundation of business acumen, some common sense, and "street smarts."

You have probably heard about famous startups that have devised and executed great ideas. This section examines how global companies like *Airbnb*, *M-Pesa*, and *Uber* began with simple yet groundbreaking ideas. Each identified a gap in the market and created solutions that redefined their industries, proving the immense value of ideation.

Airbnb

The founders created an alternative to hotel accommodation for visitors by simply putting air mattresses in a spare room, offering a homemade morning meal, and calling it an "air bed & breakfast."

M-Pesa

The founder found an easy and safe way to make mobile money transfers happen in Kenya, where roads and banking systems are lacking.

Uber

One day, the founder was waiting too long for a taxi and thought of creating a platform for easily ordering a taxi anywhere and at any time.

The stories of *Airbnb*, *M-Pesa*, and *Uber* illustrate that great ideas don't need to be overly complex—they need to address real problems. Entrepreneurs can create solutions that resonate globally by focusing on simplicity and relevance.

Of course, ideas are not limited to business or technology domains like these examples; they can be used to improve or disrupt any aspect of life.

Ideation and Creation flow into each other. First, there has to be an idea from which you create a solution. In developing the solution, think of something with the foundation of a business model.

If you're hoping to be the brains behind the next big idea, you should embrace this lifestyle! Take time for creative brainstorming and find a group of friends or colleagues who can validate your ideas.

So, think along these lines:

- What businesses do you admire? What would you do differently if given a chance to run a business you admire?

- What are the main challenges you, your friends, or your community face? What product or service do you think could address such a challenge?

Another way is to look at businesses and understand their target market and who they ignore. Businesses ignore potential consumers in one of two ways:

- By not considering a particular demographic who need their services as not a potential target or

- Offering services or products at prices beyond the reach of a particular group of people

So, if you're a business owner, thinking this way would also be how you eventually disrupt yourselves instead of being rendered redundant by youngsters who can think outside the box! A good business stands the test of time.

Once you find a viable one (or two), you can use the time to research the related market and analyze what existing players and competitors are doing. You could even write a brief business plan, run some initial customer preference surveys, and maybe even put together some intro slides for potential partners or investors.

And it would be best if you grasped that to be successful in living such a lifestyle, you must let go of the fear of failure. Fear stifles creativity, and you cannot ideate or create. You must be bold and daring, believing that even your crazy ideas are worth pursuing.

Benefits of This Pillar

Why is ideation so critical for entrepreneurs? Beyond sparking innovation, it is the backbone for growth, sustainability, and diversification. This section explores the tangible benefits of an idea-driven mindset, emphasizing how it contributes to personal and professional success.

The benefits of embracing the "Ideation and Creation lifestyle" will abound, not only to you but also to your community. They may include:

Ideas as Catalysts for Progress

When you push yourself to develop new ideas, focus on creating new solutions. This can help launch a new venture and propel you into the realm of great innovators. Innovation is impossible without fresh ideas, which fuel growth and keep businesses relevant in competitive markets.

Seizing Opportunities

Entrepreneurs with a creative mindset can identify and capitalize on opportunities others might miss.
It's your turn to spot an opportunity and transform an idea into something that benefits society.

Multiple streams of income

By diversifying their offerings, entrepreneurs can create financial stability and reduce risk.
You will eventually have numerous income streams if you think through and develop your ideas into a business. Who wouldn't want that? It is every entrepreneur's dream to make money from their dreams! So, keep at it!

Cultivating an ideation mindset equips entrepreneurs to seize opportunities, adapt to changing landscapes, and build diverse revenue streams that support long-term success.

How to Develop an Idea-Driven Mindset

Ideation isn't an innate talent; it's a skill that can be developed and refined. This section provides actionable steps to foster creativity, think outside the box, and generate ideas that align with your entrepreneurial goals.

- **Embrace Curiosity**: Stay curious about the world, seeking inspiration from diverse sources.

- **Adopt a Problem-Solving Mindset**: Focus on identifying gaps and envisioning solutions.

- **Collaborate and Brainstorm**: Engage with others to expand your perspective and refine ideas.

- **Prototype and Experiment**: Test your ideas early and often, using feedback to iterate and improve.

Developing an idea-driven mindset involves embracing curiosity, seeking collaboration, and experimenting. Nurturing these habits will position you to generate innovative and impactful ideas consistently.

As a serial entrepreneur, I've been involved in many ideation activities. Many ideas saw the light of day as real products (mostly in tech, like apps and web platforms). Not all have succeeded, but rapid failure and iteration are always integral to the creation process.

I am currently taking a course on finding new inspiration as part of my Stanford program. It emphasizes that we need to think radically and generate many ideas to generate a few workable ones.

This is perhaps the process most good entrepreneurs use, whether they pause to realize it or not!

If you feel stuck in your creative ideation process, here's the link to a FELS article[1] that can help you get "unstuck" and rekindle your inner creative streak to get those great ideas flowing again: https://my-fels.life/2020/08/25/getting-unstuck-6-ways-to-get-you r-creativity-back/

Ideation and Creation is the foundation of entrepreneurship. This chapter highlighted the importance of cultivating a creative mindset to identify opportunities, solve problems, and generate value. From global success stories like Airbnb to actionable tips for developing creativity, you've gained insights into how ideation can drive progress and open new possibilities.

As you move to the next chapter, consider how the ideation principles can be applied to your entrepreneurial journey. Remember, every great venture starts with a single idea—but the key is to keep those ideas flowing.

With a solid understanding of *ideation and creation*, we'll explore the second pillar of the Flourishing Entrepreneurial Lifestyle: Self-Discovery and Improvement. Building on the creative foundation, this next chapter focuses on understanding yourself—your strengths, weaknesses, and unique capabilities—and leveraging them to fuel personal and professional growth.

---

1. https://my-fels.life/2020/08/25/getting-unstuck-6-ways-to-get -your-creativity-back/

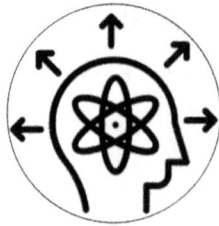

Pillar 2: Self-Discovery & Improvement

SELF-DISCOVERY IS THE FOUNDATION of personal and professional growth. Understanding who you are—your strengths, motivations, and areas for improvement—equips entrepreneurs with the clarity needed to navigate challenges, build meaningful relationships, and lead authentically. Without this awareness, it's easy to drift or pursue goals that don't align with your purpose.

The second pillar of the *Flourishing Entrepreneurial Lifestyle (FELS)*, *Self-Discovery and Improvement*, is about intentionally exploring your inner world to unlock your full potential. This journey goes beyond introspection; it's about taking actionable steps to grow, evolve, and align your work with your passions.

Self-discovery also extends to recognizing the potential in others. As an entrepreneur or leader, your ability to identify and nurture your team's strengths can elevate not only individuals but your entire business. This awareness creates a ripple effect, unlocking creativity, innovation, and collaboration across your organization.

This chapter will explore how self-discovery empowers you to find fulfillment in your work, strengthen your relationships, and achieve lasting success. By understanding yourself and embracing growth, you lay the groundwork for a more aligned, intentional, and flourishing life.

What It's All About

Having a penchant for exploring and discovering yourself introspectively, identifying strengths and areas for improvement in areas such as talent, resilience, emotional intelligence, and strength of character. Also, having a good sense of discovering and polishing others' talents and putting the right talents in the right places to unlock their maximum potential.

One of the simplest ways to begin this journey is to seek feedback from others or engage with psychometric and emotional assessments. These tools can provide fun and insightful glimpses into your latent skills, preferences, and emotional tendencies—things that may be difficult to recognize. Done thoughtfully, they serve as mirrors that reflect aspects of yourself that can guide your choices and growth.

Self-discovery also involves finding out what truly motivates and excites you. When you identify the ventures or activities that resonate deeply, you gain clarity about where to channel your energy and passion. This alignment often leads to a sense of flow—a state where work doesn't feel like work but becomes a meaningful pursuit. In these moments, you're not just productive—you're fulfilled.

But self-discovery isn't limited to understanding yourself; it extends to recognizing and nurturing the potential in others. This is a vital skill for entrepreneurs, especially those in leadership roles. Identifying talents within your team, polishing them, and placing them in roles where they can excel creates a powerful ripple effect. As a CEO or team leader, you become a *connoisseur of talent*, weaving together a diverse tapestry of strengths that elevate the collective potential.

Ultimately, self-discovery lays the groundwork for both personal and professional alignment. It's about more than just knowing yourself—it's about growing intentionally, evolving continuously, and inspiring others to do the same. By unlocking your potential and helping others unlock theirs, you create a foundation for long-term success and fulfillment.

How It Looks Like in Everyday Life

What does self-discovery look like in practice? This section explains how self-awareness manifests in daily actions, from decision-making to nurturing relationships.

Key aspects of applying self-discovery include:

- *Knowing your preferences and articulating them confidently in various scenarios:* Self-awareness yields self-acceptance. Once you understand and accept yourself, you become more comfortable and unapologetic about your choices.

- *Incorporating self-care routines to recharge and maintain balance:* You know your limits regarding how much you can exert yourself and know what activities bring you calm or rest.

- *Striving for constant improvement by embracing feedback and learning opportunities:* A self-aware person is always keen on exposing themselves to the knowledge and ideas that will transform them into a more effective person and leader.

In everyday life, self-discovery is about actionable habits—knowing your boundaries, taking care of yourself, and committing to personal growth.

Benefits of Self-Discovery & Improvement

Why invest time in self-discovery and improvement? This process is not merely a luxury for entrepreneurs—it's a necessity. Self-discovery is the compass that helps you identify your strengths, align your goals, and chart a path forward with confidence. By understanding who you are at your core, you gain the clarity needed to focus your energy where it matters most, enabling you to lead more authentically, make better decisions, and connect deeply with others.

Self-discovery is not a one-time event—it's a continuous process of reflection and intentional growth. As you uncover new insights about yourself, you also unlock a hunger for improvement. Whether through identifying untapped talents, embracing failures as learning opportunities, or fostering stronger relationships, self-awareness equips you with the tools to navigate the challenges and opportunities of entrepreneurship more effectively.

Beyond personal clarity, self-discovery empowers you to recognize and nurture the potential in others. As a leader, your ability to identify your team's unique strengths and place them where they can thrive is a powerful advantage. A self-aware entrepreneur not only builds a strong foundation for their success but also amplifies the collective success of their organization.

This section highlights the tangible advantages of self-discovery, including how it enables you to find your flow, forge meaningful relationships, and cultivate a mindset that hungers for growth. The benefits extend far beyond personal satisfaction; they lay the groundwork for professional excellence, emotional balance, and lasting fulfillment.

∞ Ability to Flow in Your Zone

Self-awareness means that you can invest your time and effort in activities that suit your personality. Then, you can enter the "flow" state, where work happens naturally as a passion.

Becoming a Connoisseur of Talent

Surprisingly, self-awareness also enables you to be able to glean into the talents and attributes of others. As a founder, you must hire people to complement your skills and talents. Your company is more of a tapestry of all the talent available in your team. A self-aware founder can select invaluable talent and place them in positions that unlock their potential.

Ability to Forge and Maintain Meaningful Personal and Work Relationships

Only a self-aware person can generate meaningful connections. Such a person can give as much as they take and become capable of comprehending the myriad consequences of their actions and words. Addressing tensions between yourself and others and mediating between others is an added benefit of self-awareness.

😊 Being Happier

Too many stories abound about the lonely, constantly worried, and depressed entrepreneur. While entrepreneurship can be stressful, no one is required to internalize the stressful aspects of the journey. With a strong sense of self, you can waddle through it all—bad days and good ones—pursuing your ultimate dream. Look at Oprah, for instance; she has gone through highs and lows, achieved much, and failed publicly. Although she openly talks about her failures, she doesn't allow them to define who she knows herself to be.

📊 Having a Hunger for Success

Self-aware people desire success and feel that they deserve it! By delving deeply into their emotions and taking charge of how they respond to their environment, they become more energetic, eager, and passionate about transforming many aspects of their lives and communities to correspond to their truth.

The benefits of self-discovery go beyond self-awareness—they empower you to work smarter, build stronger relationships, and achieve personal happiness.

Self-discovery and improvement are at the heart of the entrepreneurial journey. By understanding yourself and committing to growth, you unlock the ability to align your goals, collaborate effectively, and cultivate balance in your life.

This chapter has shown how self-awareness impacts everything from decision-making to relationships, setting the stage for more profound personal and professional success.

\With self-discovery as your foundation, the next step is leveraging continuous learning to stay adaptable and innovative. Chapter 3 will guide you through cultivating a mindset that embraces curiosity, new knowledge, and the pursuit of excellence—key ingredients for thriving in a competitive and ever-changing world.

Pillar 3: Continuous Learning

CONTINUOUS LEARNING IS THE foundation of personal and professional growth, driving innovation, adaptability, and long-term success. In an ever-changing world, where industries evolve rapidly, the ability to learn consistently sets thriving entrepreneurs apart from those who merely survive. Entrepreneurs confidently navigate challenges and seize opportunities by staying curious, seeking new knowledge, and refining skills.

The third pillar of the *Flourishing Entrepreneurial Lifestyle (FELS)—Continuous Learning*—is about cultivating a mindset of growth and exploration. It goes beyond simply acquiring information; it's about embracing curiosity, broadening perspectives, and applying knowledge to solve problems creatively. Lifelong learning empowers entrepreneurs to remain relevant, foster resilience, and inspire others by becoming thought leaders in their fields.

Continuous learning isn't limited to books and courses—it encompasses every interaction, observation, and experience that expands your understanding of the world. From engaging in inquisitive conversations to drawing insights from diverse disciplines, this habit enhances personal fulfillment and professional impact. It also unlocks the potential to share knowledge through teaching, mentoring, and thought leadership, amplifying its benefits and creating a ripple effect in your community.

In this chapter, we'll explore why continuous learning matters, how it shapes entrepreneurial journeys and practical ways to embrace it in daily life. Committing to learning and growth builds a strong foundation for success and cultivates the flexibility and vision needed to thrive in a constantly changing world.

What It's All About

It's about continuously seeking and acquiring knowledge through study, reading, curiosity, and inquisitive conversation. This goes together with a drive for thought leadership and a love for sharing knowledge with others through teaching or mentorship.

Examples of Individuals Who Embody This Principle

Brian Grazer (https://x.com/briangrazer)

You may have read Brian Grazer's famous book, *A Curious Mind: The Secret to a Bigger Life*. The book is about how Grazer rose to become a successful Hollywood producer by having curious discussions. He met people in prominent positions and learned from them. Try to become a thought leader at something you do well and share your knowledge along your journey.

Trevor Noah (https://www.trevornoah.com)

In an interview titled *Trevor Noah by the Book*, Trevor shares his love for books. He states that he loves to read to understand society's problems and because the show *Daily Show* requires him to be well-read. Trevor is a comedian and a very eloquent speaker. His understanding and explanation of issues can be credited to his time reading books!

Robin Li (http://ir.baidu.com/management/robin-li)

The richest man in China embodies the rags-to-riches story. He attributes his great success to his love of books and studying, primarily during his academic years.

Benefits of Learning Continuously

Continuous learning is more than just a habit—it's a cornerstone of entrepreneurial success. Committing to lifelong learning unlocks opportunities to grow personally and professionally. This section explores the key advantages of continuous learning and how it empowers you to innovate, lead, and adapt in an ever-changing world.

Knowledge is Important!

Continuous learning underpins all the other lifestyle points. Think about it: without taking the time to learn, there is nothing meaningful you can do or achieve. In this day and age, knowledge and skills are super accessible and affordable. With platforms such as Udemy, Coursera, and online learning platforms set up by premiere universities, there is so much you can learn!

You Become a Thought Leader

Being a thought leader means building a personal brand as an authority in a particular field. The ripple effect of such an image will be that people will trust your business as an extension of your personality. Trust will increase sales, which will grow your company and your profits. In addition to the advantages you get for your business, as an individual, you get a great sense of satisfaction knowing that people rely on you to understand our time's complicated issues.

The famous fictional character Sherlock Holmes once explained the components of his incredible reasoning powers as keen observation, sound logical deduction, and a wide base of precise general knowledge. That last part is critical to turning market observations into thoughtful deductive solutions!

As I apply this to my life, I try to broaden my knowledge base as much as possible and from various sources. I try to read 15-20 informative books per year, some of which you can find in my selected reading list. Many fields, such as biohacking, astrophysics, and advanced psychology, may seem unrelated to my work. Still, I find all of them useful, as they all come together to help me make sense of the world.

I also watch TED talks and documentaries/series on platforms like Netflix and YouTube. Besides, I don't miss a good chance to learn directly from people through inquisitive conversation.

I'm equally keen on imparting the knowledge I gain through my blogs[1] and writings, open talks, workshops, or directly mentoring and coaching entrepreneurs. This is a satisfying opportunity to expand and refine my knowledge through feedback and interactions.

This chapter emphasized the importance of continuous learning as a cornerstone of entrepreneurial growth. By staying curious and committed to learning, you equip yourself with the tools to innovate, adapt, and lead effectively in a dynamic world.

With the foundation of continuous learning established, we now turn to the fourth pillar of the *Flourishing Entrepreneurial Lifestyle*: *Travel and Exploration*. In the next chapter, we'll explore how stepping out into the world can expand your perspective, spark creativity, and fuel your entrepreneurial spirit.

Pillar 4: Travel & Exploration

TRAVEL IS ONE OF life's most transformative experiences, offering far more than leisure or escape. It becomes a powerful tool for growth, creativity, and inspiration for entrepreneurs. Stepping out of your familiar surroundings opens you to new perspectives, cultures, and a deeper understanding of the world. These experiences spark fresh ideas, reveal unique solutions, and broaden your horizons like nothing else.

The fourth pillar of the *Flourishing Entrepreneurial Lifestyle (FELS)—Travel and Exploration*—encourages entrepreneurs to embrace adventure, curiosity, and the opportunities that come from venturing beyond their comfort zones. Travel fuels innovation by exposing you to diverse geographies, histories, and ways of thinking. It's a remedy for stress, a spark for creativity, and a bridge to becoming a global citizen—an invaluable mindset today.

In this chapter, you'll explore how travel can transform the way you approach life and business. Through real-world examples and insights, you'll discover how venturing into the unknown can ignite new ideas, strengthen your adaptability, and inspire you to elevate your personal and professional journey.

What It's All About

A love for travel and adventure, understanding different cultures, geography, topographies, and motivations, embodying the global citizen and digital nomad lifestyle.

I have been to more than 95 countries and still have a long way to go.

Travel is useful for expanding your cultural horizons and enabling you to understand people's different motivations in other parts of the world.

Not everyone is built the same in how to observe things and solve problems.

Travel is also as good as medicine for the soul! It is a good remedy for stress, anxiety, and depression, improving mental and physical health.

As an entrepreneur, you can be inspired by how other people and cultures have solved their problems and succeeded. Cultural and racial appreciation are essential for entrepreneurs because we serve everyone, we serve humanity, and we need to understand society.

In this age, there is an opportunity to embrace a form of the digital nomad lifestyle. This is a big part of my own life as I manage a travel blog[1] and also produced a dedicated eBook[2] on the mindset benefits of travel. Take a look and see how explorative travel could add value and inspiration to your life!

---

1. https://aimansadventures.blog/

2. https://aimansadventures.blog/globalistas-ebook/

Examples of Successful Entrepreneurs Who Value Travel

Logan Green (https://x.com/logangreen)

The co-founder of Lyft combines entrepreneurship with his zeal for transport. Logan loves to travel for inspiration and practical reasons. While traveling, he discovers ways to improve his company and solve consumer problems. He continuously amends his business model based on his experiences on the road.

Tim Ferriss (https://tim.blog/about/)

Tim is an entrepreneur and businessman extraordinaire who lives in San Francisco and is known to travel extensively. Could his travel habits be why he saw the opportunity to be an early-stage start-up advisor and investor in Uber, Facebook, StumbleUpon, and Evernote, among others? Also, perhaps his delving into foreign languages (including Chinese) will help him with his global business dealings and spotting hidden gems!

Importance and Benefits of Travel

Travel isn't just an escape—it's an opportunity to grow, learn, and gain fresh perspectives. For entrepreneurs, it is a gateway to cultural understanding, creative inspiration, and personal transformation. This section delves into the profound benefits of travel, illustrating how it enhances communication, fosters patience, and cultivates open-mindedness, all while fueling your entrepreneurial journey.

Expand Your Cultural Horizon

People have unique characteristics due to their language, history, geography, and values. Learning about different cultures enriches your mind and soul. Entrepreneurs serve humanity; therefore, you should travel to understand the people you intend to serve.

Inspiring

The magic of travel is that it brings you to new scenes and experiences. Novelty stimulates the mind to think up new ideas and new perspectives. After a trip, you return to your business and may find it easier to think up fresh ideas that disrupt existing ones.

Enhances Communication Skills

Traveling to different parts of the world and dealing with new cultures and people will cause you to expand your scope of communication, whether in verbal or body language. You'll be required to think of alternative/creative ways of communicating away from your norm!

Builds Patience

Being outside your comfort zone helps build your character and tolerance. It may even push you to acquire new skills to navigate and successfully interact with the variables in your new environment.

Open-Mindedness

Travel will compel you to shed limiting assumptions about people of other cultures or races, helping to dispel any inherent biases or stereotypes.

A digital nomad lifestyle is rapidly becoming a global trend. People can work from anywhere in the world and become global citizens. With the advancement of technology, travel has become easy and organized, and countries have become much safer and easier to navigate.

Travel and exploration are powerful tools for personal and professional development. Venturing into the unknown expands your perspective, ignites creativity, and uncovers growth opportunities.

This chapter highlighted how travel becomes a critical component of the *Flourishing Entrepreneurial Lifestyle when approached with curiosity and intention.* It's not just about visiting places—it's about transforming your experiences into insights and strategies that drive success.

With the mindset of exploration established, we now turn to the fifth pillar of the *Flourishing Entrepreneurial Lifestyle: Using the Right Tools.* In the next chapter, we'll explore how leveraging the right resources and technologies can amplify your productivity and help you achieve your goals more efficiently.

Pillar 5: Using the Right Tools

IN ENTREPRENEURSHIP, THE TOOLS you use can be the difference between inefficiency and success. The right tools streamline operations, boost productivity, and help you focus on innovation and growth. They're not just conveniences but essential assets that empower you to meet challenges head-on.

The fifth pillar of the *Flourishing Entrepreneurial Lifestyle (FELS)—Using the Right Tools*—is about selecting resources that align with your goals and enhance your efforts. From project management platforms to marketing analytics, the right tools enable you to work smarter, save time, and achieve greater impact.

This chapter explores the value of leveraging tools effectively, providing practical examples to help you maximize your potential and thrive as an entrepreneur.

What It's All About

Using the right tools is more than keeping up with technology; it's about finding the resources that align with your goals and amplify your ability to succeed. Entrepreneurs prioritizing the right tools position themselves for better organization, improved decision-making, and enhanced performance.

Finding and using the right tools (products, devices, hacks, software, etc.) for the right purpose. Discovering hacks or shortcuts to get things done in the shortest amount of time.

Starting a business is daunting. Many fail because of the diverse skills and experiences required to create and sustain a successful new business. However, certain tools, especially information technology, are essential to gaining a sustainable edge. The benefits include saved time, lower costs, and smoother operations overall.

You're expected to stay ahead of your schedule, respond to emails, manage teams, ensure your website is functioning, organize projects, and keep in touch with your network. Luckily, there are many resources to help you simplify all of that. The trick here is to select those that will add value to your business, not just buy all the available things.

In addition to tools, there are useful "hacks" and tricks you can learn and adapt to circumvent obstacles or create shortcuts in your work routine.

The foundation of using the right tools lies in their ability to align with your objectives, simplify your workflow, and make your entrepreneurial journey more efficient and impactful.

Staying abreast of technological advancements allows entrepreneurs to remain competitive and forward-thinking. By integrating emerging trends into your strategy, you position yourself as a leader in your field.

Examples of Tools Entrepreneurs Need

To get the most out of the available tools, focus on those that address critical areas of your business. From marketing to project management, these tools streamline operations, save time, and allow you to concentrate on strategic growth.

1. Marketing tools

Since the average person spends approximately five hours daily on their phone, you may need to invest in your business's mobile marketing tools. Some tools you need for mobile marketing are push notification tools, SMS, or in-app messages. Marketing tools also help you gather valuable data on your client's behavior and give you insights to amend your strategies to suit client interests and behaviors.

Other useful marketing resources include email and social media toolkits, which you can find abundantly online.

2. Content Management System

A content management system provides an essential opportunity to manage your web presence independently without repeatedly needing external developers.

Research shows that 97% of consumers visit a company website before visiting a store or company's physical presence. Most judge the overall quality and professionalism of the business based on its appearance. My websites are mostly based on *WordPress*, but other similar platforms exist.

3. Google Analytics

As a human race, the challenges we have faced in this year, 2020, have shown the importance of tech tools a leap forward. More than ever, entrepreneurs must understand how visitors use their websites and apps. Google Analytics helps you draw insights on which pages are useful for your site visitors, which ones aren't, how many of your visitors buy your products or services, and how many. I use this currently for all my sites.

4. Working with Certified Professional Employment Organizations

Many small and medium enterprises embrace an emerging trend, partnering with Professional Employment Organizations (PEOs/CPEOs). Such partnerships allow your business to tap into industry experts and talent you would otherwise not afford. PEOs also help your business comply with local tax requirements and offer employees competitive employee incentives and benefits.

5. Freelancer Search and Hire Platforms

Another critical tool you can use in your business's early stages is outsourcing the talent you need from platforms such as Fiver or Upwork. Such platforms provide a wide pool of freelancers vetted and rated by past clients, with a simple dashboard to manage all their work and payments. I have an army of freelancers worldwide who cost-effectively manage my work without needing full-time staff or offices!

6. Project Management Tools

Project management tools like Trello allow you to monitor a decentralized team's performance. It consists of a board where you can develop cards according to the tasks at hand, assign tasks, mention specific team members, insert links and documents, etc. With project management tools, you also invest in a team chat application that connects your employees and gives you a platform for communicating and engaging on company goals.

These examples highlight how specific tools can address different needs within your business, from reaching your target audience to managing teams and analyzing performance. Effectively incorporating these tools can significantly enhance your ability to scale and succeed.

Using the Right Tools is an essential pillar of the entrepreneurial lifestyle. It enables you to maximize efficiency and focus on what matters most. This chapter explored the importance of selecting tools that align with your goals and provided practical examples to guide you in optimizing your processes. By leveraging these resources, you empower yourself to work smarter and achieve greater results.

Having explored the power of tools, we now turn to the sixth pillar of the *Flourishing Entrepreneurial Lifestyle*: *Following Technology Trends*. The next chapter will examine how staying ahead of technological advancements can help you innovate, adapt, and maintain a competitive edge in a rapidly changing landscape.

Pillar 6: Following Latest Technologies

TECHNOLOGY IS THE ENGINE of innovation, constantly reshaping industries and redefining the way businesses operate. For entrepreneurs, staying ahead of technological advancements is not just a competitive advantage—it's a necessity. Understanding and leveraging emerging trends allows you to adapt quickly, make informed decisions, and differentiate your business in a crowded marketplace.

The sixth pillar of the *Flourishing Entrepreneurial Lifestyle (FELS)—Following Latest Technologies*—highlights the importance of being a forward-thinker. It's not merely about keeping up with gadgets and software but about integrating cutting-edge solutions that align with your goals and unlock new possibilities. Entrepreneurs can harness technology to create impactful, future-proof strategies by staying curious and informed.

This chapter explores how staying updated on technological trends can empower you to innovate, adapt, and lead. With practical tips and inspiring examples, you'll discover how technology can elevate your entrepreneurial journey and position you as a leader in your field.

What It's All About

Keeping up with the latest technologies goes beyond knowing about new gadgets or software—it's about understanding the principles and trends shaping the future. This knowledge enables entrepreneurs to adapt quickly, make informed decisions, and differentiate their offerings from competitors.

> *Finding and using the right tools (products, devices, hacks, software, etc.) for the right purpose. Discovering hacks or shortcuts to get things done in the shortest amount of time.*

To leverage the right technology, you must be abreast of what is happening in the tech world, such as quantum physics, nanotechnology, space discovery, robotics and drones, biotech artificial intelligence, machine learning, blockchain, virtual and augmented reality, etc.

The assimilation of all these things in your mind will give you the edge, as you can readily draw upon new principles and follow emerging trends. This can help you participate in shaping the world's future and differentiate you from what "normal" businesses are doing.

Staying abreast of technological advancements allows entrepreneurs to remain competitive and forward-thinking. By integrating emerging trends into your strategy, you position yourself as a leader in your field.

How to Keep Up with Technological Releases

Keeping up with the fast-paced world of technology requires intentionality and access to reliable sources. This section will explore practical methods for staying updated on the latest tech trends.

- *Subscribe to industry blogs and newsletters:* Signing up for feeds such as *PopSci*, *TechCrunch*, *Wired*, etc., may prove useful. You will receive industry best practices, opportunities, industry development news, and more.

- *Keep up with the open-source community:* Trend topics in open-source communities are an excellent way to understand current issues and technologies. Starred issues on *GitHub*, for instance, can give you an idea of the next big thing in the tech world.

- *Watch some online videos:* Platforms such as *YouTube* or *Netflix* provide extensive information through documentaries on various subjects. Watching tech-related documentaries is the right way to understand trends, their history, and catalysts for change.

- *Browse social media:* Consider the following scientists and people. They are always on the cutting edge of new technology in your area of interest. If you do some research, I am sure you will come across podcasts and *YouTube* channels you can subscribe to, listen to, and get a sense of the upcoming shifts.

By subscribing to industry blogs, engaging with open-source communities, and exploring online resources, you can stay informed about technological innovations and apply them strategically to your business.

Why You Should Keep Up with the Latest in Tech

Understanding and leveraging emerging technologies is no longer optional—it's necessary for entrepreneurs aiming to succeed in today's competitive landscape. This section highlights the key benefits of staying updated on technological advancements.

New technologies are released at a staggering rate. Often, the not-so-great ones are hyped. The more superior technologies become the purview of specialists and industry experts.

As an entrepreneur, you shouldn't fall into the trap of only knowing about hyped-up technologies. Others will more rapidly pick up on these and lose their edge.

Therefore, entrepreneurs need to be intent on this for the following benefits:

- *Staying relevant:* Customers demand that businesses deliver personalized experiences at every step of the journey. Adopting new technologies that provide accurate insights is the only way to achieve such an intimate understanding of customers.

- *Competitive edge:* Embracing new technology also gives companies a competitive advantage, as it helps tiny startups and small businesses outwit and disrupt big established corporations. Examples of this dynamic abound in various emerging fields, such as FinTech, EdTech, Biotech, and many others.

- *Integration and differentiation:* A fair understanding of the technologies available allows you to integrate new technology into your business model and offer more advanced and cost-effective services than your competitors.

Over the last seven years, I've regularly attended top global tech conferences to understand what technologies are rising or fizzling out. These can be a mix of expos, tech shows, hackathons, pitching competitions, etc. You can visit this link for more details and photos: https://aimankabli.com/tech-events/.

I sometimes participate in some of these events as a speaker or mentor to interact with new entrepreneurs and hear their perspectives. This has boosted my ability to coach and advise startups, drawing upon all the fresh knowledge of what the world is doing.

Keeping up with the latest technology ensures you stay relevant, gain a competitive advantage, and integrate advancements into your business model to deliver innovative solutions that stand out in the market.

Following Latest Technologies is a critical pillar of the entrepreneurial journey, emphasizing the importance of staying informed and adaptable. This chapter explored practical ways to track advancements, highlighted their benefits, and underscored how embracing technology can set you apart in an ever-evolving world.

After understanding how technology drives progress, we move to the seventh pillar of the *Flourishing Entrepreneurial Lifestyle*: *Healthy Lifestyle Habits*. The next chapter focuses on nurturing physical and mental well-being to build the foundation for sustained success and resilience.

Pillar 7: Healthy Lifestyle Habits

Entrepreneurship is a demanding journey that requires sustained mental clarity, physical stamina, and emotional resilience. To navigate its challenges successfully, entrepreneurs must prioritize their health, not as an afterthought but as a foundation for peak performance. Healthy lifestyle habits are not just about appearances or fitness goals but about fueling your mind and body to perform at their best.

The seventh pillar of the *Flourishing Entrepreneurial Lifestyle (FELS)—Healthy Lifestyle Habits*—emphasizes wellness's critical role in achieving success. Simple practices such as eating well, staying active, and getting quality sleep can significantly enhance your ability to think clearly, make better decisions, and maintain focus during tough times. These habits are the bedrock upon which entrepreneurial grit and resilience are built.

In this chapter, we'll explore practical strategies to integrate healthy habits into your routine and discuss how even small, consistent changes can yield significant results. By nurturing your physical and mental well-being, you empower yourself to thrive in business and all areas of life.

What It's All About

Healthy lifestyle habits go beyond appearances—they're about fueling your mind and body for optimal performance. Entrepreneurs face unique challenges that demand a clear mind, sharp focus, and sustained energy. Habits like eating well, staying active, and getting quality sleep are essential to a flourishing lifestyle.

> *Healthy lifestyle habits that support mental clarity and performance include healthy eating, physical fitness, and sound sleep.*

Mental clarity and performance are the most important things to focus on. Weight management also benefits entrepreneurs, though I recommend maintaining a lifestyle that promotes mental sharpness and physical comfort.

It may be challenging to keep up with diet fads, some of which may or may not work, but the point is to make marginal changes that significantly impact your well-being. The best are simple improvements you can make consistently, as consistent effort matters.

One example I recommend is the *Bulletproof Diet* by Dave Asprey[1] . As a biohacker, he designed this diet to boost maximum mental performance for busy entrepreneurs, with possible weight loss and body definition as extra effects. The diet aims to maximize healthy fats and reduce inflammatory carbs (in some ways similar to the

---

1. https://www.bulletproof.com/diet/bulletproof-diet/bulletpro of-for-beginners/

popular Keto diet), with an additional focus on eliminating toxins that can rob us of our best physical and mental performance.

Building a healthy lifestyle starts with small, consistent changes significantly impacting your mental and physical well-being. Focus on habits that support mental clarity, stamina, and resilience.

Examples of Healthy Lifestyle Habits

What do healthy lifestyle habits look like in practice? This section includes actionable strategies for maintaining mental sharpness, physical fitness, and overall well-being.

- *Good sleep quality:* Not enough sleep can impair judgment and movement. According to WebMD, it can also make you less able to concentrate, reason, and solve problems with balance and elegance!

- *Diet and Hydration:* As stated earlier, proper diet and hydration involve optimizing your diet to support mental clarity, focus, and decision-making. Good proteins, healthy fats, and fiber are important because they counter the adverse effects of carbohydrates. Fiber also helps with digestion and waste removal from your body.

- *Exercise and hydration:* Drink plenty of water and work out to elevate your heart rate for at least twenty minutes each day. Your exercise routine should be something you enjoy and can stick to for the long haul.

Good sleep, proper nutrition, and regular exercise are the cornerstones of a healthy lifestyle. These habits help you maintain focus, make better decisions, and build the stamina needed for the entrepreneurial journey.

Value of Healthy Lifestyle Habits to FELS

Why are healthy habits so critical for entrepreneurs? Beyond physical health, they directly impact your ability to think, generate ideas, and stay competitive. This section highlights the transformative power of maintaining a healthy lifestyle.

- ***Ever seen a dumb entrepreneur?***[2] Every entrepreneur needs to be mentally at the top of their game. Your business and all other aspects of FELS are based on how your mental game is! Healthy habits mean that you can develop ideas, pursue your interests, and set up your business to out-compete your competitors.

- ***Grit***[3] ***:*** Every successful entrepreneur will tell you, " You need grit!" It would help to have the mental, emotional, and physical stamina to pursue your dream. It will not be comfortable, and many factors can pull you down or away from your goal. Do not allow yourself to be one of your stumbling blocks! For more on this concept, check out Angela Duckworth's book[4] , which is of the same title.

As I focus on researching and practicing these topics, I've put together a sort of nutritional journal[5] where I keep pictures and comments on various foods I encounter. I've also devised a quirky

---

2. https://angeladuckworth.com/grit-book/

3. https://angeladuckworth.com/grit-book/

4. https://angeladuckworth.com/grit-book/

5. https://aimankabli.com/nutrition-blog/

quiz[6] to test basic nutritional knowledge. Try taking it and discover the neat trick of solving it with just a pen stroke! Here's the link: https://aimankabli.com/nutrition-quiz/.

Healthy habits are not only personal but integral to entrepreneur success. By prioritizing your health, you strengthen your ability to innovate, persevere, and lead with grit.

Healthy Lifestyle Habits are vital for sustaining the mental clarity and physical resilience required for entrepreneurial success. This chapter explored the importance of small, consistent improvements in sleep, nutrition, and exercise and showed how these habits directly enhance one's ability to perform at one's best.

With a strong foundation in healthy lifestyle habits, we move to the eighth pillar of the *Flourishing Entrepreneurial Lifestyle*: *Strong Spiritual Depth*. In the next chapter, we'll explore how cultivating purpose, empathy, and self-awareness can enrich your entrepreneurial journey and create a lasting impact.

---

6. https://aimankabli.com/nutrition-quiz/

Pillar 8: Strong Spiritual Depth

ENTREPRENEURSHIP OFTEN PUSHES INDIVIDUALS to their limits—mentally, emotionally, and even spiritually. Beyond strategic thinking and technical expertise, entrepreneurs need a deep sense of purpose and grounding to weather challenges and maintain their drive. Spiritual depth becomes invaluable in this context, offering a source of inner strength, clarity, and inspiration.

The eighth pillar of the *Flourishing Entrepreneurial Lifestyle (FELS)—Strong Spiritual Depth*—is about connecting with something greater than yourself. Whether through faith, gratitude, empathy, or acts of service, spirituality provides entrepreneurs a foundation for emotional resilience and a deeper reason for pursuing their goals. It helps anchor you amid the highs and lows of the entrepreneurial journey, transforming setbacks into lessons and victories into opportunities for gratitude.

This chapter will explore how cultivating spiritual practices can enhance one's ability to stay centered, maintain perspective, and approach work with greater purpose. By grounding oneself in practices that align with one's values, one can create a life and business fueled by ambition, meaning, and intention.

What It's All About

Spiritual depth is about connecting with something greater than yourself, whether it's through faith, a cause, or an act of service. It's a way to channel empathy, gratitude, and compassion into meaningful actions that keep you grounded and focused.

> *Substantial spiritual depth and practice (per one's faith or preference), empathy and compassion, and a drive to serve one's nation and society.*

I am not here to advocate for any specific faith. Spiritual depth helps keep one grounded in whatever one pursues.

It would help if you had a way to vent your spiritual side. This side can be expressed in different ways, such as compassion, gratitude, empathy, or community service. It can also simply belong to an idea, thought, or movement.

Find something that suits your faith or natural preferences because having consistent and meaningful spiritual practices will keep you from burning out. Spirituality will also give you a deeper reason for doing what you do. Money is essential, but you soon find it a fickle motivator.

Spirituality adds depth and meaning to your entrepreneurial journey. By embracing practices that align with your faith or preferences, you create a foundation for resilience and purpose.

Examples of Spiritual Practices

Spiritual practices don't have to follow a specific path—they are personal and adaptable to your unique journey. This section highlights practices that can help entrepreneurs stay balanced and inspired.

Again, I am not advocating for any particular spiritual practice. All I am doing is sharing ideas to get you thinking on your terms about what may or may not work for you. Here are some spiritual practices that you should embrace as part of your FELS lifestyle:

Meditation

I think of meditation as the effort I put into adjusting the emotional impact of events in my subconscious. Did you know that 90% of people live in their subconscious mind, not their conscious mind? Did you also know that the subconscious mind controls 90% of your behavior?

Meditation is an opportunity to release the emotions attached to negative experiences that influence your daily decision-making. It also helps you be mindful of your environment and relationship with everything about being 10% happier through meditation!

Gratitude

An ungrateful person lives a sour life! Be grateful for what you have, especially if your business is not going as well as you thought it should.

Count the things that are going well and cultivate deep gratitude for them. This is the easiest way to build hope in difficult times and the best way to remain centered and focused in good times. Being grateful also helps you maintain positivity and hope.

Entrepreneurship can be heartbreaking. You may wonder if your product will be accepted, your idea will stand the test of time, or something else. Finding something to be grateful for will keep you grounded and motivate you to think about, plan, and pursue your next move. Be grateful always!

Volunteering

Think of this as anything you do for other people. Regularly allocate time, say once a month, to an activity focused on benefiting someone other than yourself. Service to others is underrated, and it feels good to do something for others! Try empathizing with people you encounter and putting yourself in their shoes.

Find practical and meaningful ways of cultivating an awareness of who you are, your values, and your moral compass. Whatever comes out of such an exercise will help you remain grounded and reap the benefits outlined in the next chapter.

Spiritual practices, such as meditation, gratitude, or volunteering, can help one maintain perspective, positivity, and a sense of purpose when facing challenges.

Benefits of Spiritual Depth

Why is spiritual depth so crucial for entrepreneurs? Beyond grounding you, it offers tangible benefits that enhance your emotional resilience, decision-making, and courage. This section examines the key advantages of cultivating a strong spiritual foundation.

Peace

People who have achieved meaningful spiritual depth are super peaceful! They have a balanced temperament and can gently express disappointment or pleasure with compassion and understanding. Peace enables you to live a life that is above your emotions. For the entrepreneur living the FELS way, your success is based on how you handle your feelings. Peace is like a navigator and the stuff that makes up your instinct. With practice, you will find that you will always enjoy following through with the decision that gives you peace and avoids that which is likely to steal your peace.

Courage

Courage separates the wheat from the chaff :) By default, an entrepreneur is not risk-averse. You dare to dream greatly and make bold moves. But you indeed cannot find courage if you do not take time to build your spiritual depth. Suppose you don't take time to build your spiritual depth… in that case, every seemingly bold decision you have made is foolhardy, and you only got lucky!

Wisdom

In simple terms, understanding is correctly applied knowledge. It kind of ties up the chapter very neatly, doesn't it? Only through wisdom can you make smart, balanced, and enduring decisions.

Spiritual depth brings peace, courage, and wisdom—qualities that empower entrepreneurs to handle challenges gracefully, take bold steps, and make enduring decisions.

Strong Spiritual Depth is an essential pillar of the entrepreneurial journey, offering a deeper sense of purpose and a foundation for emotional resilience. This chapter explored how spirituality, whether through gratitude, meditation, or acts of service, helps entrepreneurs stay grounded and focused. By cultivating spiritual depth, you enhance your ability to navigate the highs and lows of entrepreneurship with balance and grace.

With a strong spiritual foundation, we move to the ninth pillar of the *Flourishing Entrepreneurial Lifestyle*: *Open and Balanced Mindset*. The next chapter explores how cultivating openness and maintaining balance can help entrepreneurs make logical decisions and thrive in dynamic environments.

Pillar 9: Open & Balanced Mindset

ENTREPRENEURSHIP THRIVES ON INNOVATION, adaptability, and the ability to make sound decisions under pressure. An open and balanced mindset is essential for navigating these demands effectively. It encourages curiosity, embraces diversity, and rejects biases, fostering clarity and creativity in problem-solving. With this mindset, entrepreneurs can approach challenges with logic and fairness, crafting elegant solutions that stand out.

The ninth pillar of the *Flourishing Entrepreneurial Lifestyle (FELS)—Open and Balanced Mindset*—highlights the importance of staying receptive to new ideas while maintaining equilibrium in your thoughts and actions. By cultivating this perspective, you position yourself to embrace novelty, make better decisions, and lead with integrity. An open mindset allows you to see opportunities others might overlook, while balance keeps you grounded and focused on long-term goals.

In this chapter, we'll explore how openness and balance shape entrepreneurial success, offering practical strategies to help you cultivate these qualities. Adopting this mindset empowers you to innovate, build stronger relationships, and navigate challenges with poise and creativity.

What It's All About

An open and balanced mindset encourages you to embrace novelty and sound logic while rejecting biases and unnecessary conflict. Think of yourself as an artist—open to inspiration, untainted by prejudice, and focused on balance and elegance in your creations.

> *An open mindset is attracted to novelty, sound logic, good ethics, balance, and elegance and rejects biases, intolerance, and useless bickering.*

Entrepreneurship is about novelty, creating things that didn't exist before... but you must apply sound logic to achieve this. Reject anything that has to do with intolerance and bickering. This will make you more refined and elegant in the solutions you devise.

Maintain your focus on balance and elegance. You are like an artist. Artists are not biased and see only beauty and symmetry in everything. Their open, creative minds enable them to think about balancing things, designs, and colors and producing captivating art.

An open and balanced mindset transforms how entrepreneurs perceive challenges, fostering creativity, fairness, and a logical approach to problem-solving.

How to Maintain an Attitude of Openness and Balance

Cultivating openness and balance requires intentional effort. This section offers practical strategies for developing these traits, such as fostering a growth mindset and seeking diverse perspectives.

- *Growth Mindset vs. Fixed Mindset:* Foster a mindset of boldness and accepting challenges, putting in whatever effort it takes to make things happen. Learn to celebrate your failures, accept tough feedback, and reject any negative thoughts that may arise.

- **Listen more than you speak:** Ever heard the adage, listen more and talk less? Openness and balance are only achievable if you can do this! You need to be able to hear people out instead of being quick to respond to what they have to say. Listen deeply to understand their thoughts and feelings.

- **Reject biases:** Set aside time for introspection and ask yourself, "What are my prevailing biases in my career, relationships, and associations?" Bias may cause you to stereotype, that is, attribute behaviors or qualities to a particular group. Types of biases include gender, religion, race, and cultural preferences, among others. Embracing the FELS way will help you shed some of your biases. To let go of prejudices, you need to broaden your perspective, something you can do by upholding your continuous learning, explorative travel, and spiritual depth. Read more about these important concepts in this FELS article (https://my-fels.life/2020/09/04/keeping-an-open-mind-how-to-reduce-implicit-biases/).

- **Good ethics:** Having a high moral standard is another way to create balance. With good ethical standards, you wouldn't wrestle with yourself or others over a decision because you already know what needs to be done. Ethics is also a key hallmark of leadership… doing the right thing at the right time and for the greater good of humanity.

- **Seek diverse opinions:** Sometimes, you build a team so cohesive that you begin to see the same things in the same way. To avoid losing balance, seeking diverse opinions from people outside your team is essential. To achieve balance within your team, consider taking on the role of the contrarian boss, who always challenges the team to think outside the box.

- **Be comfortable with mistakes:** Always make them, whether they're your own mistakes or others. With your team, reward people who go out of their way to seek new opportunities or try new ways of doing things, even if they fail at first. Apply the same principle to yourself by being patient when trying new things that don't initially work out how you expected.

Maintaining openness and balance is about listening, challenging biases, and encouraging diverse viewpoints. These practices help create an inclusive and innovative environment for yourself and your team.

Benefits of Openness and Balance

An open and balanced mindset is not just a personal asset—it's a catalyst for entrepreneurial success. This section highlights the key benefits of embracing this mindset in business and leadership.

You Become Susceptible to Good Ideas

You do not need to pluck the next big thing from the moon! All you have to do is be open to realize and act on the opportunities around you. The balance, on the other hand, is about taming your desires and any of your excesses. Balance enables you to make smart decisions and is an exercise of wisdom.

You Can Build and Maintain a Winning Team

People respect leaders who are respectful and have an open, balanced demeanor. With that mindset, you can build a great team and fire up their motivation over the long haul toward a common goal.

You Gain Reliability

You become dedicated to those who are around you. You will also be confident in making decisions and forging new partnerships, among others, because you will have a track record, as evidence to yourself, of creating smart and sound decisions.

Being a Fair Arbiter of Disagreements

When there is contention among your team or on your board, people around you will trust you as an impartial arbiter of disputes. You will be at the center of your business because everyone will trust you with their ideas, vulnerabilities, and fears.

The benefits of openness and balance extend to building trust, maintaining a winning team, and making sound decisions. By fostering these traits, you position yourself as a leader who inspires confidence and creativity.

Open and Balanced Mindset is a crucial pillar of the entrepreneurial lifestyle. This chapter emphasized the importance of embracing novelty, rejecting biases, and maintaining balance in decision-making. By cultivating these traits, you enhance your ability to innovate, lead with integrity, and build lasting relationships.

With an open and balanced mindset, we move to the tenth and final pillar of the *Flourishing Entrepreneurial Lifestyle*: *Diverse Hobbies and Activities*. In the next chapter, we'll explore how engaging in diverse interests can fuel creativity, enrich your life, and provide a well-rounded perspective for your entrepreneurial journey.

Pillar 10: Diverse Hobbies & Activities

ENTREPRENEURSHIP IS A DEMANDING path, often requiring intense focus and long hours. However, stepping away from work and engaging in diverse hobbies and activities is essential to sustain creativity, productivity, and resilience. These pursuits are more than just a break—they challenge your mind, spark new ideas, and provide a much-needed reset to approach challenges with fresh energy and perspective.

The tenth pillar of the *Flourishing Entrepreneurial Lifestyle (FELS)—Diverse Hobbies and Activities*—highlights the importance of exploring interests outside your professional routine. Whether through adventurous sports, artistic endeavors, or endurance challenges, these activities stretch your boundaries, inspire innovation, and foster balance in your life. They remind us that growth doesn't always happen behind a desk—it often happens in moments of exploration and joy.

This chapter will explore how incorporating hobbies into your life can enhance creativity, boost productivity, and enrich your entrepreneurial journey. By stepping out of your comfort zone and embracing diverse activities, you unlock a well-rounded, flourishing lifestyle that fuels both personal fulfillment and professional success.

What It's All About

Diverse hobbies and activities allow you to stretch your mind and body in ways that your day-to-day tasks might not. They provide an opportunity to explore new perspectives, build resilience, and, most importantly, have fun. Whether you try an adventurous sport, appreciate the arts, or take on endurance challenges, these activities can act as positive distractions that lead to creative breakthroughs.

> *Diverse hobbies and activities can challenge the mind to stretch further and reach greater heights. They can also offer fresh inspiration while you are off your normal tasks. Having a little fun doesn't hurt either!*

This can be done in any form. For example, I have done some modestly extreme sports that stretch me out of my comfort zone… I have done base jumping, flown a tiny plane, and gone indoor skydiving.

Anything you do that presents a positive distraction and stretches you a bit can help. It gets you out of your normal working place, which gives you room for inspiration to strike! Many entrepreneurs find solutions by doing something outside their regular business routine, sometimes gleaning new creative ideas from the activity itself.

Engaging in hobbies and activities outside your routine helps you reset mentally and find inspiration in unexpected places. They are more than distractions—they enrich your entrepreneurial journey.

Examples of Diverse Hobbies and Activities

Incorporating hobbies into your life doesn't need to be complicated. The key is to find activities that resonate with you, challenge your limits, and bring joy. This section highlights several activities that can profoundly impact your mental and physical well-being.

- *Physical activities:* You should incorporate anything that physically engages you into your lifestyle. Fun sports like go-karting, flying a small plane, running, and other adventure activities are useful for getting your feel-good juices flowing.

- *Endurance challenges:* Have you ever soaked in a bath full of ice-cold water or held a plank for 10 minutes? Endurance activities (done cautiously) can help you build the physical and mental fortitude you need as an entrepreneur.

- *Arts appreciation:* The arts are full of beauty and elegance! Immersing yourself in any form of art, such as visiting museums, watching fine-art theater shows, or even learning/playing musical instruments, has a calming effect that clears the mind. Exploring arts and music from different countries or styles for the novelty effect is even better.

- *Electronic entertainment:* Distractions can also occur indoors. For example, computer and video games, especially those where you need to search for things or solve puzzles (not the ones with mindless shooting or similar), can help you develop your focus and precision while offering new problem-solving perspectives.

These hobbies, from physical challenges to creative pursuits, allow you to recharge, gain fresh perspectives, and improve your mental and emotional resilience. Choose activities that excite and inspire you.

Examples of Entrepreneurs with Diverse Hobbies and Activities

Many successful entrepreneurs incorporate hobbies into their lives to stay engaged and inspired. This section shares examples of notable figures using hobbies to challenge themselves and fuel their creativity.

- ***Tim Ferris*[1] :** Every week, Tim takes time to learn a new skill and then teaches his audience through a show he calls the Tim Ferris Experiment[2]. He has taken time to learn Jujitsu, motorbiking, professional poker, and drumming, among other things. What a way to keep your mind challenged and engaged.

- ***Lewis Howes*[3] :** He is a renowned handball sportsperson, public figure, and entrepreneur. Besides being an athlete, Howes also engages in an ice bath, an activity known to improve physical and mental endurance.[4]

These examples demonstrate that hobbies are not just pastimes—they are integral to staying motivated, maintaining balance, and driving creativity in both personal and professional life.

Benefits of Embracing Diverse Hobbies and Activities

Why should entrepreneurs prioritize hobbies and activities? Beyond providing fun and relaxation, they enhance creativity, boost productivity, and build resilience. This section outlines the tangible benefits of adopting diverse interests.

Enhances Creativity

By the way, you are only as impressive as the activities you do. Suppose all you do is sit around watching television all day. In that case, you are likely uninteresting ▨. But to become exciting and develop creative ideas, take time to do exciting things!

Boosts Productivity

The energy you need to be productive increases as you expend energy on fun and engaging activities. Give it a try. When you are stuck on a project or problem and unable to make meaningful progress, go outside and do something fun and exciting. That will get your heart pumping. Nine out of ten times, when you return to your project, you will have a burst of energy and ideas to take it to the next level!

Hobbies and activities enhance creativity, problem-solving, and productivity. They are vital components of a balanced, flourishing lifestyle.

If you want to explore some of my activities that are seemingly unrelated to my work, you can check them out at https://aimankabli.com/memories/! You can also find links to my collection of rare global music and some of my other multimedia hobbies.

Diverse Hobbies and Activities are the final pillar of the *Flourishing Entrepreneurial Lifestyle*, offering a pathway to personal growth and creative renewal. Engaging in exciting and challenging activities unlocks fresh perspectives, enhances productivity, and creates a well-rounded approach to entrepreneurship.

We have explored all ten pillars of the *Thriving Entrepreneurial Lifestyle* and are now moving toward concluding the journey. The next section will tie these pillars together and reflect on integrating them into one's life and pursuing a lifestyle of fulfillment and success.

Personal Stories from Global Business Leaders Living the Flourishing Entrepreneur Lifestyle

THE JOURNEY OF ENTREPRENEURSHIP is as unique as the individuals who undertake it. While the *Flourishing Entrepreneurial Lifestyle (FELS)* principles provide a framework for success, the ways these principles manifest in real-life stories are as diverse as the entrepreneurs themselves. Learning from the experiences of others can offer invaluable insights, fresh perspectives, and a sense of shared purpose.

This chapter delves into personal stories from global business leaders who have embraced the FELS philosophy. These individuals, from various industries and cultural backgrounds, share how the ten pillars have shaped their entrepreneurial paths. Through their successes, challenges, and lessons learned, you'll see how FELS principles can create balance, purpose, and sustainable growth.

These stories are a testament to the FELS framework's adaptability and universality. Whether they embrace continuous learning, leverage technology, or cultivate an open mindset, these leaders demonstrate how the FELS pillars empower entrepreneurs to thrive, no matter where they are or what they do.

As you read these accounts, consider how their experiences align with your journey and how the insights they've shared might inspire you to take the next step toward flourishing as an entrepreneur.

Abdulaziz Al Jouf

I am from Saudi Arabia

What I do: CEO & Founder of MENA's Premier Fintech Company; Serial Entrepreneur, Fintech Influencer; Coach and Mentor, Bookworm, Fitness Enthusiast, a Globe Trotter and Just Really Fun to Chat With!
Find me on:
  • LinkedIn: linkedin.com/in/abdulaziz-aljouf

Every Obstacle Is a Hidden Opportunity

Open and Balanced Mindset

I BELIEVE IN BEING ambitious, persevering, and never giving up on anything, be it a business idea or a dream. I'm one of those who thinks when the going gets tough, I should get tougher!

My life has always been filled with challenges. However, I have learned to wake up, face each one head-on, and never give up. I always look at obstacles like challenges—they were meant to be overcome.

Continuous Learning

I firmly believe in taking chances and making the most of the opportunities. One of the first things I learned through my experience is that you cannot do it without money since operation costs are inevitable.

Self-Discovery and Improvement

First, you must work smarter and elevate your mindset to embrace entrepreneurship.

Secondly, you cannot do it without a good team. Building a good team is the second most formidable challenge for an entrepreneur. However, it is the most critical since a good team can make or break your business.

A good team will build on your ideas and improve the quality of your decisions as a leader. I always surround myself with what I call a challenger (a person who doesn't fear challenging their boss).

Lastly, do not fear change but embrace it. The people who ultimately succeed in life are not the strongest or the most intelligent but are adaptable to change and survival. It's always about moving to your next destination without delay. Change is part of the journey, so why the fear?

Other pillars that have contributed to my life and success:

Ideation & Creation, Travel & Exploration, Following Latest Technologies.

Additional Thoughts and Advice for Upcoming Entrepreneurs

- Wake up before dawn to make the most of your 24 hours to plan, execute, and implement your thoughts and ideas. Early birds are known for meeting their goals.

- Hire and work with people you haven't worked with before and learn from their diverse cultures. A multicultural team will amaze you! Always choose a team that will negate your weaknesses by their strengths!

- Remember, just like in business, you are the CEO of your life. Hire, fire, and promote those you want in your circle.

- Have fun. It's essential, especially for Gen Y & Z.

- Be an avid reader. Try to read at least one informative article daily, learn from it, and pass the knowledge on to your team.

- Great ideas often start in a Starbucks coffee shop or on a napkin! Traveling opens your eyes and doors to new possibilities and will expose you to new, exciting adventures you wouldn't otherwise dare—at least, it does for me.

Abdulrahman Alkhodair

Abdulrahman Alkhodair was a visionary entrepreneur and consultant from Saudi Arabia whose journey exemplified the transformative power of travel and exploration. Driven by a passion for embracing new cultures and ideas, Abdulrahman lived abroad for several years, broadening his perspective and redefining his approach to entrepreneurship. His experiences in Canada inspired him to create Pitch 'n 'Close, a business that helps entrepreneurs refine their pitching skills to better connect with investors.

Abdulrahman believed that stepping out of one's comfort zone—whether through travel, change, or challenging traditional ways of thinking—was key to personal and professional growth. His life's work and philosophy continue to inspire others to embrace diversity, innovation, and the courage to live boldly.

What May be Wrong for You, May Be Right for Others

Travel & Exploration

IN 2009, I MADE one of the most important decisions of my life. I have never regretted it, and I don't think I will ever regret it.

I left my very good job, which had great benefits, and went to Canada to pursue my education. In my first years in Toronto, I learned more about expressing myself and my feelings without embarrassment.

Later, I became aware of the meaning of more than one truth. I knew this meaning before, but I didn't live it. However, living in a multicultural country, in a city that is the heart of this country, made me experience and live this meaning. What might be true for you may not be true for others; what is wrong for you might be the right belief for others.

However, I'd like to share a story about Ideation and Creation. Since I was in Saudi Arabia, I wanted to start a business. However, my way of thinking was a traditional one. I wanted to open a Beauty Salon for women. I reasoned that women tend to pay without thinking, so I'll have a business that targets women. However, during my studies in Canada, I learned that starting a business must come from a problem that a business could solve for a specific target customer.

So, I started exploring different people's needs and ideas. Then, the Dean of Entrepreneurship College guided me to visit and attend a gathering for investors and experts in the entrepreneurship world. During this gathering, I learned that investors have pain and that entrepreneurs don't focus much on pitching their ideas to investors, so I decided to start a business that helps people with that skill. Here is where *Pitch 'n 'Close* started.

After living abroad for several years and seeing others living outside, what I might advise others to do is, for the sake of whatever is holy, don't hang out with people from your culture. Because that way, you can't learn a new culture, you won't open your mind to new people, you can't experience a new way of thinking. You can't say you've lived abroad and learned from being there if you only knew people from your country.

Don't be afraid of change. It might take some time. Some people change quickly, some in a long time; that doesn't matter. What matters is not being afraid of change, embracing it, and living it. You only live once, so live it fully and make it count.

Annie Duke

I'm from Texas, USA

What I do: Speaker, Author, Student of Decision Science

Find me on:
- LinkedIn: linkedin.com/in/annie-duke

Choice and Luck, That's All You Get!

Continuous Learning

WE ARE ALL LEARNERS, and as learners, we interact with information from the world. Unfortunately, for most of us, new information comes in to certify the blues that we may be experiencing.

In other words, we're ossifying or hardening our beliefs and mental models about the world, as opposed to approaching new information open-mindedly. We often fall into the danger of using new information to reinforce false beliefs, inaccuracies, and limiting mental models.

I believe only two things determine the level of success we'll find in life—the quality of your decisions and luck. Luck isn't something you can change. It's something that happens to you. So that means you have to focus on the quality of your decisions since it's the only thing you can control.

To improve the quality of your decisions, you must upgrade your beliefs. You must discover who you are and be essentially yourself, your world, and your mental models; these are the things that inform your choices. Every person should be focused on the foundations of their beliefs, repair the cracks, and correct the inaccuracies.

Information acquired through learning is the foundation of beliefs, so continuous learning is essential to me. I have learned to approach further information with a pretty open mind to understand what I need to know and what I need to unlearn, and at the base of that is a very Bayesian mindset.

Using the Right Tools

You see why having the right decision tools is so incredibly important. Unfortunately, I have observed that some people are kind of enamored with the idea of making decisions based on their gut. It's as if they have some magical quality that makes them think you can just wing it and get to a better place.

I have found that one of the advantages of using tools for decision-making is that they help mitigate any bias you may have. Further, an excellent tool enables you to replicate the right decisions and expect to get more similar positive outcomes. A useful decision tool will help with that creativity and those insights that you have to express in the world in a way that's going to increase success.

An excellent tool allows you to replicate the decision and expect to get more similar positive outcomes.

The other thing about having the right tool is that it allows you to examine your decisions like objects in retrospect. You know we're making all sorts of decisions.

Then, the world gives us some feedback about those decisions. It is useful to be able to look back and say, "What was I thinking at the time? What tools did I apply? How was I working through this decision?" And now that I've learned all this new information, would I have made the same decision again? What can we learn from it?

Taking time to reflect on and assess past decisions will prepare you to make even better decisions in the future.

Healthy Lifestyle Habits

I'm a vegan who works out daily and doesn't drink a lot. I realized that my physical self is connected to my psychological and intellectual self. As an ardent poker player, I know from poker that people have this image of a poker player, an overweight person smoking a cigar with a Visor, but that's not true.

Most of the top poker players are mostly pretty healthy. It's because poker is mentally exerting, and you need to be mentally and physically at your top game if you're to compete well. If your physical self doesn't feel right, your emotional self isn't going to feel good, and your intellectual self isn't going to feel good. You'll find it challenging to apply your knowledge of the game.

That is why, at the base of everything, I strive to have my physical self as healthy as possible. When I am in good health, I can trust that my perspectives on issues are balanced and that my ideas have a greater chance of success. For me, this is something incredibly important.

Bob Brotchie

I am from Cambridge, England

What I do: Life Coach, Psychological Therapists, and Managing Director at Anglia Counselling based in the UK

Find me on:
- LinkedIn: linkedin.com/in/icefounderbobbrotchie

- Instagram: instagram.com/bobbrotchie/

Anglia Socials:
- Website: www.angliacounselling.co.uk/blog/

- Facebook: facebook.com/angliacounsellingnewmarket

My Success Is About the Impact of My Life and Work

Self-discovery & Improvement

I HAD A TRAUMATIC childhood, suffering multiple abandonments and emotional neglect, which led to extremely poor academic attainment. But, realizing the tools and choices associated with self-discovery and improvement proved to be a fundamental driving force for disproving the limitations others placed on me.

Continuous Learning

I was 27 before I truly began to comprehend and then realize just what I could be capable of achieving in life. At 27, I started a successful and award-winning career in front-line emergency medicine that would see me operating on land and in the skies as a paramedic.

I also rose through the managerial and leadership ranks via my desire for continuous learning.

During this career, I discovered an innovative bent that had lain dormant. While still a paramedic, I created the tech solution, the *In Case of Emergency* (ICE) process for mobile phones, which subsequently gained worldwide acclaim![1]

Travel & Exploration

I have enjoyed world travel, most of all when traveling solo, on business, and for pleasure. I spent many months in North America, with shorter periods in North Africa, SE Asia, and Europe. Isn't traveling the best way to learn from other cultures?!

The most significant life lessons I continue to appreciate and derive value from are those I have learned through studying Buddhist Philosophy, specifically mindfulness and meditation.

---

1. https://en.wikipedia.org/wiki/In_Case_of_Emergency

I have suffered and burned through stress, and my introduction to mindfulness became the conduit for not only recovery but sustainable resilience. Little did I know then that I would eventually, some ten years later, begin to teach the ways of 'presence' and 'being' via non-attachment. We must recognize and choose a new relationship with the inevitable suffering we will all face on this earthly planet!

These newfound skills also allowed me to separate from the 'all-consuming' pressures of emergency medicine and management and formulate a plan to take what I had learned from suffering and share it with others. I created a new chapter to become a counselor – and entrepreneur.

Success for me is now, perhaps more than ever, derived from that which I can impart to others. To facilitate this, I choose to take great care of my psychological and physical well-being. I enjoy staying active, creating space to 'be' studying, spending time with my family, and practicing meditation. I no longer simply live to exist. Now, I live and thrive, fulfilled via a meaningful and purposeful life serving others and myself.

Cali Yost

I am from the outskirts of New York City

What I do: CEO and Founder of the Flex+Strategy Group, a strategic work flexibility solutions company

Find me on:
- LinkedIn: linkedin.com/in/caliwilliamsyost/

Make What Matters to You Happen Every Day

I THINK ALL TEN are essential, but if I had to pick the ones with the most influence, it would be the following and all equally as I believe they are all mutually reinforcing and inter-related:

- Ideation and Creation

- Self-Discovery and Improvement

- Healthy Lifestyle Habits

- Open & Balanced Mindset

- Continuous Learning

- Strong Spiritual Depth

In the early '90s, I was about five years out of college and a junior manager in training at a bank. I started to suffer from chronic headaches and stomach issues. Doctors couldn't pinpoint the cause, and various treatments didn't work.

Finally, I stepped back and realized I needed to change my high-stress lifestyle.

This realization started me on a 25-year journey of physical, emotional, and spiritual development that directly contributed to my professional and personal success over the years.

Another tip or hack I'd like to share is this: I follow the advice outlined in my book *Tweak It: Make What Matters to You Happen Every Day*, with the most consistent standard "tweaks" in my work+life fit being:

- Every morning for over two decades, I've meditated for at least 20 minutes and written in my journal.

- I move my body in some way every day for at least 30 minutes, whether it's weightlifting, walking, yoga, or some form of cardio exercise.

Chris Folayan

I was born in Nigeria, studied and living in the United States

What I do: CEO MallforAfrica

Find me on:
  • LinkedIn:

linkedin.com/in/chrisfolayanbusinessstrategist/

Don't Think You Can Discover Market Needs of Other Countries by Just Googling!

Travel & Exploration

YOU NEED TO UNDERSTAND the people you are selling to, and you need to understand that culture. There's nothing better than traveling and experiencing that culture and experiencing the people you're selling to. I will give you an example from myself. I was born and raised in Nigeria, did everything all the way to high school, finished high school in Nigeria, and then migrated to the States.

When I got to the States, I could see what was lacking in the environment I grew up in.

I traveled to the US and noticed the differences between how online business is done in the US, Nigeria, and Africa in general. I took that experience and created 'Mall for Africa,' which is currently in over 30 African countries. It helps people in Africa buy stuff and products from US and UK retailers.

I could do this successfully because I came from an environment that I understood well. I understood that I was trying to sell to unbanked people, had no credit cards, only local currency, and had never done anything online. There were many hurdles to overcome, and I developed a platform, which was the first of its kind, that allowed people without credit cards to purchase items from US and UK retailers.

Had I not been from that environment, had I not traveled to the US to see how things were different, then my business would never have been able to be as successful and as big as it is today. That's just one example of many, but as I've, we've expanded our business outside Africa to Latin America, Asia, and the Middle East.

Once, I traveled to Kenya and saw that the motorcycle biker industry was huge, and I wanted to do something about it. I saw it as an opportunity and started thinking about what I could do to benefit from it. So, I got more biker platforms on our platform to sell into Kenya, and that's how we could service the biker community in the country. However, I recognize that I wouldn't have known Kenya has a vibrant biker community had I not visited the place.

Travel enables you to discover different things and open your eyes to opportunities. It also allows you to understand and embrace the culture of new target markets and do first-hand market research by meeting local people and asking questions to understand their needs.

If you think you can do all this by googling, doing research, and becoming a great entrepreneur, unfortunately, you probably will not be as successful as you can be if you travel and explore.

Again, that's twofold—you travel, you review everything, you look at everything, you think outside the box, and you interview people, talk to people, get that camaraderie going, and become friends with them so they can help you with your idea, you can bounce ideas off them, and they feel like they're part of your growth. There is nothing wrong with having local mentors be part of your growth.

I have local mentors in several countries all over the world helping me out, helping our decision-making and our progress because whenever we have ideas on making changes, I call people. These are people that I've formed relationships with over the years because I traveled and met them face to face. Now, they've turned into amazing relationships, and I can bounce ideas off them because they live in these countries.

I can travel there and explore, but I only get so far. I also need to create that bond with someone locally to pass ideas to them. So, travel and exploration are huge requirements if you want to be an amazing entrepreneur.

You will not get as far as possible with your business idea if you don't travel. Just like you do market research locally whenever you have an idea, you want to run it by people to ensure this idea has wings and will do well locally. Take that same principle if you want to expose your products to people outside your country, outside your community, take that exact principle, travel, explore, meet with people, ask people questions, see if your idea is valid in that market and then take it to the next level. So again, travel and exploration are highly recommended.

If you don't do it, you may be successful. If you do it, you will be 100% more successful, which I guarantee.

Christina Rao

I am from Vancouver, Canada

What I do: Stock Market Expert

Find me on:
- LinkedIn: linkedin.com/in/socialite4finance

My Entrepreneurship Is Fueled by Connecting with Others

Ideation & Creation

A BUSINESS IS LIKE a village; its people are your tribe, with a shared purpose of creating an impactful, sustainable community.

As a serial entrepreneur, it is easy to fall head over heels, madly in love with my ideas. However, it isn't until I gain the opinions, views, and knowledge of my tribe and other tribes that I can confidently execute the best business model.

Self-Discovery & Improvement

Self-awareness is crucial for my entrepreneurial success, and it is a lifelong journey. I am forever on the quest to be and do better. I'm fascinated by human neuro functions and how much we control who we want to be. I started my entrepreneurial career in my early 20s, standing 5 feet tall, weighing 100 lbs, and being attractive.

Often, I was perceived to be a pushover and likely lacking smarts. I had to improve my confidence and rely on my smarts to have businessmen (The Old Boys Club) take me seriously. Now, 20 years later, I can walk into any boardroom and command respect. My self-discovery also helps me identify areas of my business that need adjusting to continue evolving. I use this experience to empower other young women working in corporate finance.

Using the Right Tools

Time is money; you will spend more in the long run without the right tools. A great example is my website. Ten years ago, I had my website built on a platform that wasn't mobile-compatible and couldn't be easily converted. Three years ago, I bought a website template that requires coding to be compatible with updates. Now, I'm learning to let go of how the design looks and understand the functionality.

Healthy Lifestyle Habits

Everyone's healthy lifestyle and habits are different. I found quitting caffeine seven years ago terrific. I rested better with 4-6 hours of sleep and waking up and getting focused was not challenging. Simultaneously, I gave up dairy. I didn't feel good about drinking milk meant for baby cows. These changes have given me clarity, far more energy, and focus.

Open & Balanced Mindset

We all want to feel this way. Maintaining this mindset is essential for being objective in business. An open mind prevents me from judging my own opinions, allowing me to spot stock market trends early.

Continuous Learning

Living in the digital age, nothing stays the same in business. It is imperative to continue learning for success. I am involved in many different sectors of the stock market. Over the last few years, I focused on learning about cannabis and CBD concerning medical treatments. Today. I'm learning about new technology available to the mining industry.

Travel & Exploration

Life is about experiences, not material things. The people I meet traveling and my adventures enlighten how I evolve and run my business. I have spent entire trips in historical museums contemplating the resources the artists had access to hundreds of years ago to create these masterpieces.

I have no excuses for creating my masterpieces as an entrepreneur because I have abundant resources at my fingertips—an incredible motivator and very humbling.

Following Latest Technology

Catching up with the latest tech is hard for me. I am not tech-savvy, but I like to know the latest-greatest and how I can get a slice of the pie. It's in these unicorns where millionaires are made. Having some young friends who can help you stay on the pulse of tech is a great idea.

Strong Spiritual Depth

Spiritual depth is everything. I built my business on a strong spiritual foundation. I realized that all humans are connected and that there is enough abundance for everyone. Therefore, we all need to cooperate in building communities, and everyone's role is significant.

Charity begins at home, which is an essential saying for me. Ensure those closest to you are well, and extend that care to your neighbors, neighborhood, and community. I never donate to organized charities except for animal rescues.

I'd instead feed people on the streets and make an emotional connection. I like face-to-face interactions when giving or sponsoring a hot lunch program at a school in my city.

The more you give, the more you get!

Diverse Hobbies & Activities

It's wonderful to try many things, find what you enjoy, and then find what you love. These things relax you yet challenge your mind. An unchallenged mind has no place in the world of entrepreneurs.

The more activities and classes you try, the more people you meet, and your network expands. I love dogs, and with dogs come dog walks and meeting other dogs and their owners, a new system of people in my life.

Christine Michaelis

I am from Germany

What I do: CEO and Founder of Creative Start-Up Academy and Co-Founder of European Startup Association

Find me on:
- LinkedIn: linkedin.com/in/christinethecoach

- X: x.com/TweetTheCoach

- Facebook: facebook.com/YourCoachChristine

- YouTube: youtube.com/user/ChristineTheCoach

Creative Start-Up Academy Socials:
- Instagram: instagram.com/creativestartupacademy

My Life's Constants are Change and Flexibility

Self-Discovery & Improvement

ALL MY LIFE HAS been about change, flexibility, and self-discovery.

I was born and raised in Berlin, Germany, but now, as a Digital Nomad, I live in different countries yearly, have many ideas, and run my own businesses. I have always strived to improve and wanted to help others. I now also understand that you learn and improve with every moment and experience in your life.

I didn't always see it that way. Of course, I had moments and periods when I felt lost and deflated and thought I was wasting time. After my A-Levels, I spent three years doing one internship after another, understanding what I didn't want to pursue as a career path. Back then, I thought I was wasting time by not making a decision and not knowing.

I have worked in hotels, event management companies, sports bars, printing companies, TV lifestyle magazines, and more. After a final internship at an advertising agency, I decided to pursue marketing and advertising. I completed an apprenticeship and worked in marketing agencies for over 13 years. I enjoyed scouting and shaping talents and running workshops for my colleagues during that time.

Back then, I was convinced I had found something I wanted to do for the rest of my life. But no, after ten years of working in the industry, I no longer enjoyed it.

It was not rewarding enough. I didn't feel I had enough impact or see each individual's changes. I wanted to do more, create more, transfer more knowledge, and make other people happy.

I undertook an NLP (Neuro-linguistic Programming) and Coaching certificate course, which changed my life! I found my next calling! But wait, I still wasn't too sure what to do with the knowledge and how I could help people with a specific problem. Sometimes, we have to start and see what happens. And what happened to me was that I started working with start-ups.

Of course, I still had a full-time job, which meant I worked every lunch hour, evening, and weekend to get my business running. It took a lot of dedication and hard work, but it was all worth it! I loved – and still do – working with entrepreneurs and start-ups. Their drive and passion rub off on me, and seeing the progress they are making with my help excites me, makes me happy, and gives me a sense of accomplishment. And one of the main things that keep me going on my current path is the constant improvements I go through myself. I learn from every single person I meet and work with. I continuously encounter challenges in my business – like everyone – and overcome these with curiosity, knowledge, and dedication.

However, learning new business-related things is essential to me. I have a long bucket list of things I want to learn and places I want to see. This starts with learning new musical instruments and some martial arts and goes on to dancing and much more. And as someone who wanted to have it all at once, I did all at once. My days were filled with work and hobbies from 7 a.m. to 11 p.m. But you can only go for so long with that kind of schedule.

I started to feel stressed and tired. I was also diagnosed with a brain tumor, which turned out not to be one – but you can imagine, I got even more stressed. I was very close to burnout, so I decided to take care of my body and mind and made that a priority. Doing this, I also went through changes and self-development.

These days, my drive to learn new things and improve myself has stayed at the same level, but I have learned to pace myself and take one step at a time. For example, I pick max. Three things I want to learn or improve each year for my hobbies.

I take one step, channel, and product at a time for my business. You can be even more productive if you single-task and focus all your energy on one thing at a time. In the past four years, I have published twelve books, built an online community, created multiple challenges and online courses for start-ups, worked with universities, individuals, and small businesses across Europe, and founded a not-for-profit organization for start-ups (European Startup Association).

Now, I know that all I have done has supported me in finding my way, improving myself, and leading up to what I am doing now. These epiphanies mostly happen later in life when looking back at what you have done. I always say, "If you want to do something, do it. If you want to learn something, learn it. Simple."

So my conclusion is: Never stop improving, but ensure you also care for your body and mind.

Christine Hassler

I am from Texas, USA

What I do: Keynote Speaker. Best Selling Author. Credentialed Life and Business Coach. Millennial Expert. Spokesperson

Find me on:
  • LinkedIn: linkedin.com/in/christinehassler/

The Best Investment We Can Make Is in Our Own Mental, Emotional, and Spiritual Health

Self-Discovery & Improvement

I GREW UP A very insecure child due to bullying and teasing, and I compensated for that by being a massive overachiever. I thought that my success in the world was what would make me worthy and amicable. I decided that if no one liked me or didn't fit in the world, I would be the smartest person in the room, and I was very successful.

I was a straight 'A' student in high school, which got me into a great college. I graduated from that early and then moved out, and by the time I was 25, I had a very successful career in Hollywood as the youngest female agent. However, I was driven by my insecurity and a super demanding internal voice. A voice that would constantly push me to be more successful, study all night, take the extra class, get the promotion, or whatever form of achievement was available for taking. Outwardly, I was very successful, but internally, I was very insecure, suffering from both depression and anxiety.

I was representing Hollywood writers, directors, and producers, and my boyfriend, at the time, was the head of this big movie studio. I was living the Hollywood life, Oscars and Golden Globes, hanging out with celebrities. Again, from the outside, anyone would look at me and say, wow, you have it all; internally, it was a different story.

I was good at pretending; I got good at wearing masks. But the façade began to fade when one morning, I was on my way up to my office in the elevator, and I had my first ever anxiety attack or panic attack. It was pretty scary, I didn't understand what was happening so I became confused, pacing in and out of my office. Eventually, I just started walking around the block.

As I was walking around the block, I realized I'd been miserable at my job for a long time, and it wasn't because I didn't like it. I was miserable because I never stopped to think about why I even pursued it. I was doing this job in an industry I didn't care much about. I dealt with many things I could categorize as part of the *Me Too* movement. I was dealing with harassment, though not like some people, but I was impacted by it. I was working crazy hours, and I was miserable. So, I decided at that moment I would quit my job. But I was terrified because I was the kind of person who always made plan A work.

Up until this moment, I never really needed a plan B. I didn't know who I would be without the identity of a successful job after quitting. I went into a deep depression.

From early on in my life, I struggled with depression since I was 11. I was on antidepressants from 11 until 30. I had tons of anxiety. I went into massive debt. I was estranged from my family. I was engaged, and 6 months before the wedding, my fiancé broke up with me.

So, at the very right age of 25, everything crashed down. I was seeing a life coach, but I wasn't listening to everything she was saying. One day, I had this moment on my bathroom floor where I realized I was the common denominator in everything in my life. So, since I created chaos in my life, I can create something different. I remember returning to my coach and picking up some personal development books. I decided that I would no longer be a victim of my life, and that's when personal development became my passion.

The passion turned into purpose, leading me to write my first book called *20 Something 20 Everything*. When I was in the thick of things, I was looking for a personal development book to help me with what I was going through, and I couldn't find any.

The writing journey also led to me coaching and counseling people, and I started speaking on stages from colleges to corporations. I became an expert on millennials, which led me to get a master's degree in psychology, lead massive retreats, speak on more stages, and write. I wrote two more books, and now I have a highly successful, thriving business in personal development and a fulfilling personal life.

When I was 11, and they put me on antidepressants, they said you have a chemical imbalance; you will need these for the rest of your life, and I believed them. Now, I'm not anti-antidepressants, I'm not anti-medication. I think it's a personal choice; for some people, it is necessary. I'm just speaking of my experience.

I always thought I needed them, but around my late 20s, when I started to get into personal and spiritual development, I realized that I was numbing myself from a lot. I made the empowering choice to get off them and have been off of them for more than a decade now. I feel alive and not numb, and even though sometimes I get sad and sometimes angry, I also feel so much joy and contentment.

I would say work on yourself. Childhood, no matter who you are, impacts everything about you. It impacts how you see the world, your decisions, the people you attract into your life, your relationships, and your attitude toward money.

Get a coach or get a therapist to help you unpack your childhood. To help you understand your model of the world, your biases, and your limiting beliefs and to teach you how to heal, manifest, and make things happen.

It all starts with changing your mindset; I've always said the best investment we can make is in our mental, emotional, and spiritual health. I train life coaches and work with many entrepreneurs, and many people pursue entrepreneurialism because they want to feel fulfilled and fill a void. Just like my success was first fueled by insecurity, that fuel eventually runs out. Meaningful and holistic success only comes when they are peaceful and healthy internally.

I started exercising in my teens and have continued throughout my life. I don't exercise for weight loss or vanity. I do it because it gives me clarity, keeps me youthful, and gives me that edge that I need.

It's a healthy way to get adrenaline. I think I see it with a lot of entrepreneurs. They are looking for the adrenaline rush in their business and become so work-addicted that they completely forget about their bodies. So, exercise is massively important, and eating the right foods is massively important. Your business won't thrive unless you're thriving. I don't eat processed food. I prioritize making sure that I'm exercising and eating well.

In the morning, I do breathwork, EFT tapping, meditation, or a combination of all the above.

At night, I do some kind of binaural beats, music listening, or a gratitude list, something to calm me down. The first thing I'd say about a healthy lifestyle habit is sleep. Sleep is not something you can never catch up on. That's another thing I hear about entrepreneurs: I will catch up on sleep on the weekend, I'll catch up on sleep after my watch.

No! When you get some good sleep, you perform better, are more attentive, and make fewer mistakes. So, sleeping anywhere from 7 and a half to 9 hours at night is a massive priority, and it always has been for me. I always make sleeping non-negotiable.

Dave Gray

I am from Missouri, USA

What I do: Author, Consultant, Speaker, Coach

Find me on:
 • LinkedIn: linkedin.com/in/davegray

You Cannot Learn New Things If You're Unwilling to Let Go of the Old

Open & Balanced Mindset

THE MOST COMMON MISTAKE I see people make is assuming that they understand the situation. Sometimes, they see a problem one way when others see it very differently. Sometimes, other people don't see a problem at all, or they see a different issue.

I have a friend named Mick Calder. He works at a company called the 333 Group in Melbourne, Australia. Mick is a turnaround guy. If you're running a company, Mick is the last guy you want to meet because if you meet him, it means you're probably in trouble.

You meet Mick when you have run out of other options.

Once you meet Mick, his organization will offer you two alternatives. The first is that they can take you into bankruptcy. They will help you liquidate the company and help you through that choice's legal and financial aspects. The second option is that they will take the company away from you and turn it around. They will buy you out of debt, and they will own the company in exchange for taking on your debt.

Mick's company is very good at this - they have turned a lot of companies around. I was curious about this and asked Mick: "When you take over a company, you know nothing about it. While the people you are taking over from have been there for many years—sometimes as long as 40 or 50 years, and you can turn it around. Yet the people who worked there for all those years, with all of their knowledge and experience, could not do so. How is it possible that you can succeed where they have failed?"

I also asked him, "What do you do differently? How can you come in and make positive change happen so quickly?" Mick told me that when his team arrives in a company, the people who work there are ready for change. Mick and his people go in, and they listen. They talk to employees. They speak to customers. He told me that customers and employees always know what needs to be done between them.

You listen? I asked. So simple? How can that be?

Mick told me that it's rare for a team that got a company into trouble to be able to turn it around. The chances are that they were successful before they started having problems.

They had hit on something that worked well sometime in the past. But the business world doesn't stand still, and over time, things changed.

If a team has been successful for many years, they will keep doing those things that made them successful, even when they don't work anymore. When they start to fail, they will blame their failure on everyone except themselves. They get to a point where they are in denial and unable to learn. It's times like these when paying attention is the most important thing you can do.

Additional Thoughts & Advice for Upcoming Entrepreneurs

Nine practices to help you minimize reality distortion, envision possibilities, and create positive change.

1. Assume that you are not objective. If you're part of the system you want to change, you're part of the problem.

2. Empty your cup. You can't learn new things without letting go of old things. Stop, look, and listen. Suspend judgment. What's going on?

3. Create a safe space. If you don't understand the underlying need, nothing else matters. People will not share their innermost needs unless they feel safe, respected, and accepted for who they are.

4. Triangulate and validate. Look at situations from as many points of view as possible. Consider the possibility that seemingly different or contradictory beliefs may be valid. If something doesn't make sense, you're missing something.

5. Ask questions and make connections. Try to understand people's hopes, dreams, and frustrations. Explore the social system and make connections to create new opportunities.

6. Disrupt routines. Many beliefs are embedded in habitual routines that run on autopilot. If a routine is a problem,

disrupt the routine to create new possibilities.

7. Act as-if in the here-and-now. You can test beliefs even if you don't believe they are true. All you need to do is act as if they were true and see what happens. If you find something that works, do more of it.

8. Make sense with stories. If you give people facts without an account, they will explain it within their existing belief system. The best way to promote a new or different belief is not with facts but with a story.

9. Evolve yourself. If you can be open about how change affects you personally, you have a better chance of achieving your aims. To change the world, you must be.

David Burkus

I am from Oklahoma, USA

What I do: Author, Keynote Speaker, Organizational Psychologist

Find me on:
- LinkedIn: linkedin.com/in/davidburkus

The Myths of Creativity

Ideation & Creation

IDEATION AND CREATION HAVE been a big part of my work. I've written five different books, and the biggest one was my first one, The Myths of Creativity, which is about the myths and misconceptions about creativity.

There are ten myths in that book, some of which I subscribed to before I started researching it. One of the biggest ones was the expert myth or the expertise myth.

According to the myth, the more we know about a subject, the more likely we are to solve the problem using our creativity and ideation. The truth is that's not accurate. As we increase in knowledge, we increase our creativity and ability to solve problems, but only to a certain point.

The correlation then goes back down, and further expertise limits our ideation and creation. Research shows that the reason for this is that when you're coming up with ideas because you know so much, you also start to think of why your ideas won't work and end up not implementing most of them.

You need to do things to deliberately keep an open mind and keep learning about many different fields, not just the one we're getting a degree in or pursuing a career. When you look at disruptive innovations or ideation methods that add value to a company, you'll find that most companies have one thing in common: Disruptive ideas are created because people applied a concept from one field to a totally different discipline and created something new.

Most innovators start in one discipline, move to another, and apply the lessons from both to solve a problem in a whole new way. In my own life, I incorporate this in a couple of different tips and hacks. First, I'm always trying to learn about new fields, so I watch videos on YouTube.

For example, my big thing right now is trying to learn as much as possible about filmmaking and video creation, not only for my career but also because it's fun and I get to know different perspectives. We all need that; this is more than just having one hobby. It's what you do to deliberately keep track of or learn from many fields that are not your legal career.

I'm a writer and an academic by training. Producing videos and films has nothing to do with academics. But it's fun, and it makes me learn new things. I'm not exactly certain how I'll apply them down the road, but I know they'll be helpful. It always works out that way.

The other tip I have for that is to make sure that you spend time with people not in the same industry as yourself or those who don't share your worldview or political ideology. Make sure you're spending time with people who are different from you. You will learn from that that the world's a vast place with much raw material for ideas, but you'll need to get broad and keep a working knowledge of everything that's going on.

If you do that, you're much more likely to find an idea in one area that maybe you just studied a little bit. And find a way to bring it back to your field, and you'll create a ton of value for yourself and society. Remember, ultimately, the way people create value for themselves is to create value for their community first. That's always been that way. It only ever happens that way.

You don't do this by chasing expertise. You need to start with the foundation of knowledge in a specific field, push the boundaries of what you know, and keep a working knowledge of many different fields.

The best way to describe this in the research literature is as T-shaped. If you think about your experience, a vertical line, like the vertical line in the capital letter T, represents your deep level of expertise in one area.

Still, there's also a horizontal line that goes across that makes that capital letter T, and that's the idea we use for keeping a working knowledge of many other fields.

Be T-shaped. The world will shape you and let you grow in one area, but be T-shaped and keep being T-shaped.

Open & Balanced Mindset

The mindset pillar also resonates with me because I felt its ideas can be compared to the book I wrote, Friend of a Friend. The book is about how networks form, how people connect with communities, and how they interact with them. It expounds on what a network means for your professional system and how you get the things out of life, your career, or the company you want for them.

Networks form clusters; systems form tight silos around shared ideology or shared background or shared ethnicity or shared gender. People who think alike are clustered together, which is a problem - if you're around people who don't have a good enough mindset for themselves, then you will think like them. That's a problem for sure, but most systems think that even successful people can lose everything or make a terrible decision.

The leaders of businesses, companies, and governments can make horrible decisions when surrounded by people who think a lot like them. All this is in the network science literature, referred to as homophily, which clusters around the same-sided ideas, limiting your perspective. And business history is full of this, by the way.

Xerox invented the personal computer; you know that the graphical user interface that made the personal computer, whether it's Mac Macintosh or Windows, that made it possible was invented by Xerox.

They didn't develop it. Their senior leaders thought this had nothing to do with making copies of physical paper. The future is in documents, not in this thing. So, we're going to pass on it, allowing Apple and Windows to develop it underneath from underneath them and lead to a lot of financial troubles for Xerox.

Kodak invented the digital camera. The people who created that little thing on all of our smartphones now to take photos electronically were at Kodak, the most established company in making films. Still, their senior leaders, who were too clustered and all in one agreement about the way to see the world, decided that the future was in the film because it had better quality than this tiny little prototype they were being shown.

They couldn't have imagined that as technology increases the resolution, the quality of these photos would increase. Now, every one of us has a camera on our smartphone that is better quality than what a film camera could ever produce, and Kodak would have been the beneficiary of that had they seen that future.

So, the big hack or tip I have for this is that, over time, I've learned to audit my network and keep track of the people I talk to. I asked. I work with many executives and ask them to do the same thing.

I look at the last 25 people they interact with most frequently. I tell executives, "Let's get your calendar out, see who's been in the meetings you've been in over the last three months, make a list of the top 25 people you're interacting with, and then see how much different or similar they are to you."

Almost everybody ends up in a scenario where 15 to 20 of the 25 people are very similar to them because it's comfortable. We like having conversations with people who agree with us. We love people who think like us because clearly, they're brilliant.

The only problem is that we're limiting ourselves and our perspective. We do not see the whole world as it is. We see it just through this one lens shared by people with our similarities, and we end up making those Kodak or Xerox decisions. The good news is that most of us find that we're not talking solely to people we're similar to when we do this audit.

We're also talking to people we're different from, and being different from them is good news because we know that if I spend more time with that person, I'm already talking to them a little bit, but I need to invest more time with that person.

Let them introduce me to more people they know so I can learn more about their perspectives.

Then you grow much better. You learn many different perspectives. I've often heard it said that if you're the smartest person in the room, you're in the wrong place.

Still, I also think that if you're entirely comfortable with what everyone in the room is saying, you're in the wrong room because you're in a place with people who agree with you.

Instead, you should deliberately seek out conversations with people who see the world differently, and that will make you uncomfortable.

Dr. Riad Hartani

I was born in Algeria then mostly lived in San Francisco, California, and Vancouver, British Columbia, and Paris, Tokyo, and Hong Kong

What I do: Tech Nomad - Building advanced technology startups and taking them to market globally

Find me on:
  • LinkedIn: linkedin.com/in/dhartani

The Journey Is Always More Important Than the Destination

Travel and exploration

I SPENT MOST OF the 2000s and 2010s building high-risk/return Internet tech startups from Silicon Valley and other tech hubs worldwide. In doing so, an essential challenge after building high-tech products is taking them to global markets. This made me circle the world many times, working on global deployment. On some occasions, I had to visit over 20 to 25 countries in a single month.

The challenge was to adapt to different cultures, styles, habits, and ways of doing business at a very high frequency and be forced to adapt rapidly. Simultaneously, traveling to different places and meeting people helped me advance some of the startups and achieve success. Travel is also about adapting, understanding, getting an advance, and accepting. These are fundamental to an entrepreneur.

It is all about keeping the eyes wide open, feeding the mind's curiosity, and listening to all signals. It is about learning and knowing that the more one learns, the more there is to learn. Once that sinks in, the journey becomes what matters more than the destination. To make that journey fulfilling, learning to live with that sense of discovery and exploration, that feeling of jumping out of the comfort zone is paramount.

At the end of it all, it is that "Just go, see the world, and make it a better place" that fuels much of what entrepreneurship is all about. I had lived that myself and lived it through many other entrepreneur friends around me. I recently wrote a book, "Tech Nomads of the Universe," about travel and innovation across cultures and geographies. By the time I had finished writing up that book, highlighting stories around the world, I was sure of one thing: travel, discovery, and exploration are a bit like the spices of success and fulfillment. At least for me!

Following Latest Technologies

It is said that much of what one grows up with stays with him for the rest of his lifetime. I grew up in Algiers, and as a kid, there were a few TV animations that I couldn't miss. It happens that they were all about space, robots, and things at the edge of science. Animations, yes. But still, at that tech edge. It made me open up to my curiosity and made me want to get into that high-tech edge.

That ended up being the case as I went into advanced research and then built startups over time. In essence, it is that feeling of tracking the latest technologies that have been the guiding principle of what I have done over the last decades. It is about curiosity, wanting to know where things are heading, desiring to build the next thing, and, in some sense, a bit like wanting to leave in the future. Ironically, it all started with TV kids' animations!

It is all about knowing how to learn enough about some things to decide whether one wants to understand more about them. It is all about being curious enough to learn new things and favoring the "what is next" versus the "where are we today," "how it could potentially help me," and the "is it useful for me right now?" Human beings will always aim to advance technology as it fulfills that sense of exploration, discovery, and moving forward.

For some reason, it is what human ingenuity is all about. Following the latest tech has that sense of having one foot in the present and one foot in the future, and in turn, that is what gets the entrepreneurs to make that jump into the unknown. Jump first, and you will figure things out, kind of thing!

Additional Thoughts & Advice for Upcoming Entrepreneurs

The formula for success is a bit like a food recipe of sorts. There are as many formulas as there are delicious dishes out there. There is no single formula. One has to come up with his formula. Moreover, one can hardly know that formula ahead of time.

One learns it on the go, through trial and error, failure and try again, observation, and adaptation. Ultimately, one wishes he had done things differently, a bit different or even a lot different, regardless of success and prosperity. The secret is to accept what one ends up with and be happy with the outcome, knowing one has given it his best. It's harder said than done, but well, so be it!

Friederike Fabritius, MS

I am from Germany

What I do: Neuroscientist, keynote speaker, and award-winning author of "The Leading Brain: Neuroscience Hacks to Work Smarter, Better, Happier" (Random House, 2017)

Find me on:
- My website: www.fabulous-brain.com

- X: x.com/fabulous_brain

- LinkedIn: linkedin.com/in/friederikefabritius

Even Old Dogs Learn New Tricks!

Continuous Learning

HAVE YOU HEARD THE saying, "An old dog can't learn new tricks?" Well, as far as the brain and learning are concerned, it's not true. Even older people can learn; when people have trouble learning, it's usually because they used the wrong method.

Most people think that learning happens in the prefrontal cortex for rational thinking when, in reality, it happens in your limbic system, where emotions are processed.

The hippocampus, which filters incoming new information, is located in the middle of the limbic system, right between the nucleus accumbens, which processes positive information, and the amygdala, which processes negative information.

Whenever you learn something new, you have to make sure that it has what I like to call emotional relevance. What is emotional relevance? Some people learn a new language to put it on their CV because it looks good, but they usually fail with these attempts because there is no emotional relevance.

Our brains only learn when deeply emotionally involved and when what we learn matters to us. For example, I'm fluent in six languages, and I always had an excellent reason to learn them.

For example, as a student, I wanted to live in Sweden. I was living in Austria then, and I joined a Swedish choir, made Swedish friends, and learned Swedish by singing Swedish songs. By the time I moved to Sweden, I was fluent.

I learned languages in three parallel ways;

- I was working in the laboratory and exploring how the brain processes language.

- I explored the language based on my insights into how the brain works.

- I also supported myself working as a language teacher.

Sometimes, I had students who didn't want to learn. Their employer sent them to language lessons, and I was their teacher. First, I always asked, "What are you truly passionate about?"

One of my students was passionate about World War II weapons and tanks. I said, "OK. Bring your miniature tanks to our lessons, and we can talk about them in English."

Even then, this older executive who didn't want to improve his English learned because we found a topic that truly mattered to him. So, when we try to learn something, we must ensure it has emotional relevance.

Learning is not a rational process; it's an emotional one.

Jareer Oweimrin

I live in Dubai

What I do: Cofounder at Fluidmeet

Find me on:
- LinkedIn: linkedin.com/in/jareer

Be Calm, Composed, and Thoughtful

Self-discovery & Improvement

WE ALL GO THROUGH different life experiences daily. Some are more impactful than others, often leading us to reflect on how the situation transpired and what could have been different to reach an optimal ending. You do find out that small traits you never knew existed or never made it to the surface below. It's at these points where only through the proper reflection do you realize that acknowledging and recognizing that trait helps you propel your own persona's molding.

That persona is continually being tested and stressed to bring out the more improved you. That discovery of these traits begins to mesh with other characteristics you've strengthened over the years, but you'll also have to find a new balance as the order has been altered. New traits like tenacity must be balanced with persistence to ensure you're not alienating clients or colleagues.

New traits like calmness in stressful situations must find their new equilibrium with ambition.

These discoveries apply to behavioral characteristics as much as they do to knowledge and skills. As you mature into a professional adult and progress through life, you should know that time for self-discovery enables you to manage your persona and the implications of your decisions and actions.

All this happened recently to me as our business came to a screeching halt, similar to many who lived through COVID-19. Our company deals specifically with meeting and event spaces in the hospitality business, so we knew that our business would be affected.

After four years of building a business, we saw our work crumble in a matter of weeks.

We went through a reckoning during that time. What should we do, and how should we do it? A significant change was inevitable. A survival mechanism kicked in.

A defense mechanism that I never knew existed started to protrude. It was pronounced and shook the calm within. How could this dormant trait be managed while ensuring its balance with all the other characteristics that had been previously developed? I realized that handling the situation would take more than subduing it.

Suppressing the urge to react would not solve the issue. It would still require calmness, an in-depth analysis of its roots, and an assessment of the extent of its impact on other facets of my personality.

With those particular steps, I could adequately navigate the stress and manage the situation more objectively. To this day, I reflect on the importance of discovering it, articulating its importance, and resolving its placement with my professional persona.

But through all this, I learned that an entrepreneur should always - be calm and composed in action, careful and comprehensive in thought, mindful in reflection, and happy in response.

Koh Tsu Yi

I am from Kuala Lumpur, Malaysia

What I do: Marketing personnel for a Training & Development company | Confidence Life Coach

Find me on:
- Facebook: facebook.com/tsuyi

- LinkedIn: linkedin.com/in/tsuyi

- Instagram: instagram.com/tsuyikoh

Adopt a Beginner's Mindset When It Comes to Learning

Self-discovery & Improvement

IN EARLY 2017, I was forced to shut down my business. (I ran a franchise business in child supplementary education.) I was in six-figure debt, jobless, and even ended a seven-year-long relationship. It was my darkest moment in life—feeling defeated, hopeless, and helpless.

As an ambitious woman, these setbacks (that happened simultaneously) were a big blow. I lost all confidence in my ability to strive for success. Out of desperation and barely surviving, I explored various avenues, went out of my comfort zone, and did things I'd never thought I would. There were many trials and errors and endless failures along the way. I became exhausted—mentally and physically.

My body got weaker, and I began to accumulate a couple of illnesses within months. That became my awakening moment when a thought dawned on me, "how can I thrive when I can't even survive?"

Healthy Lifestyle & Habits

In that instant, I decided to commit to self-care, learning, and growth. I started my self-care regime, sought personal development mentors, and practiced everything I learned daily. The new routine and lifestyle helped me regain my strength and confidence to rebuild my life from zero. I grew from being powerless to powerful. I finally feel alive again! I have been exercising these healthy lifestyle habits consistently until today.

Continuous Learning

While I regained my health, I never stopped seeking learning opportunities. One of the highlights in my life that contributed significantly to my personal development, specifically in self-discovery and continuous learning, was attending Tony Robbins' Unleash the Power Within Seminar.

As I reminisce about this moment, I feel very grateful to have had the opportunity to participate in his live seminar. It was a fantastic experience being in a room with 13,000 other participants, where everyone had high energy and was constantly at peak state! The four-day seminar was so impactful that it created a breakthrough for me. It helped me uncover and discover more about myself while bringing more certainty to my life's goal. It was then that I decided to be a personal development Life Coach.

Subsequently, I have always sought ways to continuously improve myself by attending seminars, exploring various freelance jobs (aside from my full-time job), and enrolling in online courses. All of these have allowed me to learn at a fast pace, gain many new experiences and exposure, and broaden my network. The journey isn't always smooth.

There were times when I felt exhausted and overwhelmed by further information, yet I kept going because the only way to progress and achieve success was to take action.

Success is a journey of progression supported by a continuous learning and development process. Embrace the process and enjoy the trip.

Additional Thoughts & Advice for Upcoming Entrepreneurs

If you want to be successful, you need to be committed to your goal. The journey always starts with your way of being – adopt the right attitude and personality.

Patience, Persistence, and Perseverance are the three key behaviors that show up for me.

Be open to learning. Regardless of your status or position, adopt a beginner's Mindset when it comes to education.

Create a daily schedule incorporating self-care (such as facial, physical exercises or workouts, meditation), personal time with loved ones, reading for learning and development, and work. Ensure that your schedule is practical and useful. Its objective is to serve you and guide you to a healthy and balanced lifestyle.

Engage a coach or mentor that can support you in achieving both personal and professional goals.

Last but not least, surround yourself with like-minded people who are on a similar wavelength, if not better. This is so that you can learn and contribute to one another.

Muhammad Chbib

I am from Munich, Germany

What I do: CEO of Tradeling, the hyper-growing eMarketplace focused on business-to-business (B2B) transactions in the Middle East and North Africa (MENA) region

Find me on:
- LinkedIn: linkedin.com/in/muhammadchbib

There Is Always a Silver Lining

Self-discovery & Improvement

IN EARLY 2017, I was forced to shut down my business. (I ran a franchise business in child supplementary education). I had a 6-figure debt, jobless, and even ended a 7-years long Ideation & Creation.

I love bringing my ideas to life and seeing them positively impact other people's lives. While still at school in Germany, I first discovered my entrepreneurial spirit. When I was 12, I bought a second-hand bicycle for 40 Deutsche Marks. I did it up a bit and sold it at a 50 percent margin. That meant I could buy two more bikes, which essentially kick-started my first trading business. It taught me special skills, like how to negotiate and how to sell. These are skills that are still relevant to me today.

While I was probably the richest boy in my school at the time, walking around with hundreds of Deutsche Marks in my pocket, I knew that selling bikes wouldn't make me rich in my adult life. So, I started thinking about what to do next. With my earnings, I bought a computer and started teaching myself to program. It was more of a hobby than a business, but it held me in good stead and helped me land an office job while studying. It is a matter of being proactive, forward-thinking, and seeing your ideas through.

Many people have brilliant ideas but don't know how to see them through and bring them to market. They often give up at the first hurdle. You must fail first, which is the only way to learn from your mistakes. Failure is nothing to be scared of; I have failed many times, and each time, I have emerged more robust than ever before.

You also have to be agile. It is a critical component of any business's survival. I am an avid fan of McKinsey's Pyramid Principles, which I have applied to any company I have led. They allow you to see things from multiple perspectives and adjust accordingly.

To give you a recent example, at the start of 2020, I was ready to launch Tradeling, a brand new B2B eCommerce marketplace with a killer business model set up for success.

We were just about to launch our first two verticals, Food & Beverage and Office Supplies, and the whole world came to an abrupt halt due to the global pandemic—Businesses shut, hotels closed, and our real reason for being was no more.

I am not a defeatist. There is always a silver lining somewhere; you just have to take stock and find it. Then, it is a matter of readjusting and realigning your business to adapt. We did precisely that. We had two choices: delay our launch or adjust. We chose the more challenging route. We quickly realigned our business model and launched an unplanned vertical—health and Wellness.

We capitalized on an opportunity at the right time, creating a digital marketplace for business buyers to trade masks, gloves, sanitizers, and protective equipment. This vertical was relevant to the market realities and will be for a long time.

We had a revenue stream, and I didn't have to lay off a single person. In fact, we are snowballing because of our agility and readiness to embrace something new and see opportunities in times of adversity.

We now have more than 100 people compared to just 30 before the crisis. It is a matter of looking for opportunities and adapting to capitalize on them. You also have to make business decisions for the long term, which means being tactical, exploring revenue-generating streams, and executing them.

Additional Thoughts & Advice for Upcoming Entrepreneurs

The global pandemic has accelerated the use of eCommerce globally, and this trend will continue. Businesses must evolve with it and embrace digital transformation, or they will be left behind. At the same time, it is critical to keep the human touchpoints to ensure you don't distance yourself too much from the customer. It can create a disjoint.

Mohamed Isa

I am from the Kingdom of Bahrain

What I do: Investor, Business Advisor, Board Member, Award-Winning Speaker, Amazon's Bestselling Author, Publisher, and Tour Director!

Find me on:
- Instagram: instagram.com/mohamedisa3ds
- X: x.com/mohamed_isa
- LinkedIn: linkedin.com/in/mohdisa
- Website: http://www.3dspeaking.com

Be Curious. Be Adventurous. Be Marvelous

Self-Discovery & Improvement

I AM CURIOUS. I have loved reading since I was a child. I cannot resist books.

When I was 13, I read a Career Guide that stated the accountant commanded the highest salary.

Since then, I have decided to be an Accountant. It became my goal.

I asked my cousins and teachers about the profession. I was on a mission. I passed my Certified Public Accountant (CPA) Exams in the USA. After that, my career accelerated. At 26, I was the youngest CFO of a publicly listed company in the Gulf States.

Travel & Exploration

Since July 2016, I have been a part-time tour director for European tourism tours.

And what a way to travel the world for free! There are many rewards for such a job. I get to meet people from different walks of life and learn from them.

I collect original stories and anecdotes that I could use in my articles and speeches. I also experience diverse cultures, explore history and heritage, and look for business opportunities.

And as a bonus, I have fun in the process.

Diverse Hobbies & Activities

I enjoy creating networking opportunities for others to find employment, business ventures, and more. In November 2018, I started a WhatsApp Group for the University of Hull Alumni in the Gulf States.

Since then, we have been adding value to each other. A colleague recommended my name to join a Supervisory Board for Tech Startups in the USA. And I did. Once the business takes off, I expect a sizable financial reward.

Regardless of your beginnings and current situation, you can transform your life. I am sure you heard the term "Self-made." All of us are self-made, whether we admit it or not. We can be successful or not. It is our choice. Make the right choice.

Be Curious. Be Adventurous. Be Marvelous. You can do this!

Mohammed Madani

I am from Jeddah, Saudi Arabia

What I do: Director-General, Center of Spending Efficiency, Business Owner Best Spots Trading Establishment + spotspal app Soccer Team Coach/Leader

Find me on:
* LinkedIn: linkedin.com/in/mohammedmadani

Passion Often Leads to Purpose

Diverse Hobbies & Activities

SINCE I WAS A little boy, I have been drawn to different sports. I was very active during most of my childhood. One sport in particular that I was so attached to is soccer. I loved everything about it, but I have never been a fanatic about a team. My obsession grew with me, and later, during my career, I started organizing extraordinary soccer practices.

I took organizing to a new level using different tools; some were already available, and others I had to create from scratch. I had to learn a few things to enhance my capabilities in coding, for instance. I did this until 2012 when I discovered I wasn't really about soccer but rather my passion for organizing and guiding others. That became my business model, which I have worked on for the past few years.

In summary, I'll say:

- Find your passion and link it to your purpose.

- Embrace your areas of strength.

- Take the initiative to make the change.

- Avoid staying in your comfort zone.

Continuous Learning

I would start by giving all the credit to my father, who has always pushed me to learn new things and never claimed I didn't know the answer to his question.

Since childhood, this behavior has triggered something inside of me: curiosity. I believe it is the key to always wanting to know more.

It has become a habit that whenever I am asked a question, I don't know the answer. I hardly say I don't know but immediately look for an answer. Such behavior has broadened my knowledge and understanding of how things generally work.

Although I have three different educational backgrounds, all from decent schools in the USA, I still see the most valuable things I learned were on the go.

Always remember:

- A day passes without adding to your knowledge; it means you've fallen behind.

- The world is moving very fast; you need to keep up. Try edx.org, Coursera, Udacity, and other unconventional education platforms.

Additional Thoughts & Advice for Upcoming Entrepreneurs

Whether you want to change the world, improve your career, or start your own business, it all begins with you. You are the one who needs to take the initiative and make the first move. Think: What are the odds someone will come and give you that little push out of kindness?

Michelle Kwok

I am from Vancouver, Canada

What I do: Co-founder & CEO at FLIK

Find me on:
- Instagram: instagram.com/mkwoks
- LinkedIn: linkedin.com/in/michellebkwok
- X: x.com/michellebkwok

Medical Science Student Breaking into Entrepreneurship

Diverse Hobbies & Activities

WHILE IN UNIVERSITY, I pursued a medical science degree, encouraged by my traditionally minded family, but I felt so narrow in academics. From a young age, I knew that my family wanted me to be a doctor, but I wasn't always sure about the path.

So, I started thinking about my passions outside of school. I began to join clubs that had nothing to do with my degree, like the Sports Business Club and Right to Play, because I wanted to explore something new and some other interesting areas.

From there, my extracurricular interests expanded from videography to branding to entrepreneurship. With my videography skills, I figured I could break into content marketing. I cold-emailed brands and cool startups, asking to volunteer my time as a 'content creator' since I taught myself how to create videos and edit. I used this 'marketing' skill to get my foot in the door, then pushed the envelope in each position I received to get hired into more comprehensive-scope positions.

Between rigorous study sessions, I helped launch a digital marketing agency, worked for Bumble, developed sports business partnerships, and created events challenging GenZ strategists to take on the world's most significant issues. These "apprenticeships" I made in university allowed me to translate my experiential learning into real-world situations. I worked in everything from content marketing to events, partnerships, and product development.

Even though I was a medical science student, I probably had more business experience than business students. I started posting my story on LinkedIn, honing my one-liner as the 'medical science student breaking into entrepreneurship' and building a personal brand that opened up many non-medical opportunities.

Looking back, I can see the seemingly unrelated pieces of my puzzle coming together to form a purposeful image. Going through pre-med helped me improve my analytical thinking; learning to overcome external pressures to follow genuine passions gave me the self-confidence to pursue social entrepreneurship; being a leader at an all-girls school during my formative years showed me the global importance of female mentorship and empowerment, and my work during college allowed me to develop the community-building talents that are so key to FLIK's success.

Over the years, my diverse experiences and hobbies have played an integral role in my present and future.

Additional Thoughts & Advice for Upcoming Entrepreneurs

If you're an aspiring entrepreneur, here are some of my most incredible tips:

- You have a personal platform, so get your entrepreneurship story out there. People want to hear from you and help you. Hone your story and start building your network today—you never know who will listen and invest in taking you to the next level.

- Find a side hustle skill like I did with videography. Develop it and find ways to apply it in real-world settings. Keep pushing for new opportunities once you get your foot in the door.

- GET EXPERIENCE. Whether through apprenticeships, internships, freelancing, volunteering, etc., you need to get experience in your field or discover entrepreneurship's inner workings to take the next big step.

- Look back on your life to see what you've been passionate about and where your puzzle pieces fit. Entrepreneurship only works if you're building a solution to a problem you're intrinsically motivated to fix.

- Lastly, develop blazing confidence in yourself. If you don't believe in yourself, why will others? If you think you can do it, you WILL do it.

Nader Amiri

I am Canadian/Iranian, raised in Dubai

What I do: Entrepreneur (Founder & COO of elGrocer)

elGrocer Socials:
- X: x.com/elGrocer

- Instagram: instagram.com/elgrocer

- Website: https://www.elgrocer.com

There Is Always Another Way

Ideation & Creation

EVEN WHILE I WAS in a corporate role for over ten years before starting my entrepreneurial journey, I was always told I had unconventional methods. Just because "something didn't work before" or "that's not how we do it" never stopped me from seeking alternative ways to reach our goals.

My fond memories are how I led the team that helped establish Oreo in the GCC when it was initially 'failing' as it was not what the GCC consumer was used to seeing as a 'biscuit.' (Most customers said it is like charcoal; biscuits should not be a chocolate shell, as it makes my kids' teeth dirty).

While the company was about to delist Oreo from the region, we devised a 360-degree plan which included digital marketing (which was very new in area 15-20 years ago), shunning TV ads for over a year (which was crazy to consider as TV was the 'must' when trying to build a brand), even rebranding the packaging to highlight the 'biscuit' even more (which was counter-intuitive given customer concerns), and other strategies and tactics. Those 1-2 years were critical to building Oreo's acceptance in the region.

Eventually, the Global Oreo team called upon us to help guide all new countries launching Oreo and countries where it faced customer acceptance issues. After that, the team has done a fantastic job helping make it a mega brand, not just in North America but everywhere now!

Eventually, with the bureaucracy in corporations, I never felt satisfied and always had more ideas to explore. Hence, I started getting involved in the startup world in various ways: attending groups & conferences, helping on projects within my areas of experience, and even investing.

Till I eventually left the corporate world to start a grocer.

Don't be afraid to share your ideas; you can see/hear many different perspectives by sharing. I always like to use an example of an idea as a 'Wikipedia' page that you start and manage. People can come and edit and put their inputs, but eventually, you can shape it to be in the 'final' version you want

Just because 'this is how we do it' or 'it didn't work before' shouldn't stop you from creating and doing something from a fresh angle

Self-discovery & Improvement

Thanks to some great professors, bosses, and family over my formative year, I always thought I didn't want to become a 'dinosaur.' To do that, I had to immerse myself in learning many things and improving the ones I found more interesting. I love reading all kinds of books, from different business books to autobiographies, history, sociology, psychology, physics (time travel theories, quantum computing), and even more!

Even earlier in my career, I remember every year asking for new roles and tasks to do so I could learn more, which also helped me know more about myself... what I like and dislike, from sales to trade marketing, brand management, and innovation management, among many other broader projects. Even on the personal front, traveling, whether with friends or alone, helped me explore what and how everyone else is living and more about myself in reflective phases.

I love the Japanese philosophy of Ikigai, and having learned about it earlier, I set myself on the path of finding this equilibrium.

Read and not just one genre/type... it helps open the mind.

Meditation helps you reduce stress and clear your mind. It also enables you to see, hear, and reflect on your thoughts. Start with ease. There are no rules and no periods; just sit in silence.

⊠ Always dabble in new things, familiar and unfamiliar, to push the boundaries of your mind and experiences.

Travel & Exploration

Thanks to being in Dubai, travel is easy! I love traveling and exploring, with cities being my favored type of destination, though one of my last long trips a few years back to New Zealand changed this for me.

I must say that from all my travels, it has been my favorite destination for a long time now. My favorite story was back in 2010. We suddenly got an extra-long weekend, and based on a wager with a friend, I went on to take the next flight out, which happened to be New York.

I remember feeling that my brain hadn't processed that yet, and I remember waking up mid-flight wondering where I was and why I was on a plane!

I arrived in NYC and thought to myself, while I am here, why not go a bit further and spend two days in Los Angeles as well? It was a crazy week. Out of six nights, I was on a flight for three of them, but the Adrenaline rush was outstanding.

Explore the world! Try different destinations to see other ways people live and also your preferences.

Do some planned and some unplanned travels to keep it fresh.

Nara Iachan

I am from São Paulo, Brazil

What I do: Co-founder and CMO at Cuponeria. Experienced in marketing, passionate about communication and advertising

Find me on:
- Instagram: instagram.com/naraiachan
- LinkedIn: linkedin.com/in/naraiachan

Don't Dwell on Your Mistakes

Ideation and Creation

I HAVE ALWAYS WANTED to reinvent everything around me, thinking about new solutions and often implementing them. I don't like standardized things, and I still believe that things can be done differently and achieve better results.

I have a creative profile, which was significant at the beginning of Capoeira and is still essential for each new feature nowadays.

You don't have to accept things as they are. You may want to change them.

Focus on the goal of facilitating and improving people's lives.

Continuous Learning

We often make mistakes along the company's trajectory, which is normal. Instead of thinking about how bad the error is, I always try to get the best learning from each one.

Everything is useful for education and allows the accumulation of knowledge. Our philosophy is always to test, even with the risk of error.

Test a lot.

It's difficult, but try not to be so upset about mistakes.

Keep everything necessary for each experience. Everything can be useful in the future.

Travel and Exploration

The habit of traveling is significant in Capoeira's trajectory. We learn many habits and trends in each country we visit, especially when the coupon and technology market is more relevant. Before bringing the culture of coupons to Brazil, I went many times to countries where coupons were used a lot, and I tried to use coupons for everything: food, transportation, shopping, and others. It taught me a lot.

- Prioritize places where your market is strong.

- Interact with other entrepreneurs and other companies.

- Observe the habits of people from other places.

Following Latest Technologies

Knowing all the new possibilities is essential to providing the best for our users. Knowing all the recent technological trends is necessary to be a useful resource optimizer. We know that not using those new resources can cause financial loss and rework. I like following all the news, participating in events, and taking refreshing courses. Google (one of our investors) greatly helps us with this and always offers tools, events, and courses.

- Test all the news.

- Update yourself. Make courses, go to events, read often.

- Test the tools of your competitors.

Rania Batayneh, MPH

I am from Portland, Oregon

What I do: I am a Nutritionist and a #1 Amazon Bestselling Author of The One One One Diet: The Simple 1:1:1 Formula for Fast and Sustained Weight Loss

Find me on:
- My Website: www.essentialnutritionforyou.com/

- Instagram: instagram.com/raniabatayneh

- Facebook: facebook.com/raniabatayneh

- X: x.com/raniabatayneh

View more information on my book, The One One One Diet: www.amazon.com/One-Diet-Simple-Formula-Sustained/dp/1623360323/

It's All About Mindset

Open & Balanced Mindset

IN MY 20-YEAR CAREER as a Nutritionist and Wellness Coach, I have learned so much from my clients and readers. Ninety-five percent of my clients have the same goal - weight loss.

But everybody has a different lifestyle and different needs. Learning about each client's eating personality, diet, and weight history gives me insight into the best way to support their goals. I look at the client with a 360-degree approach. Learning how to eat right for weight loss should also make you feel more energized, satisfied, and, above all else, confident as you move through your journey.

This is why I create strategies - behaviors that you can engage in daily that will give you results now and in the long term. My focus is always on structure, not restriction. We are exposed to products and diets daily through social media. My goal is to help my clients get the clarity they need to be more open and develop a balanced wellness and weight loss mindset. (Yes, you can eat dessert and still lose weight!).

A few years before I started writing my book, I worked with pre-op bariatric surgery patients on a supervised diet and weight loss program, giving them the tools and strategies to achieve the criteria set by their insurance provider for a 10% weight loss before the surgery.

Patients who met eligibility criteria at the time of initial presentation qualified for surgery.

Patients who successfully reached their target goal weight now had clearance to have surgery.

Additionally, patients who successfully lost the 10% weight loss requirement had healthier outcomes with fewer postoperative risks associated with the surgery. Further, I continued consulting with patients post-op to ensure compliance with the dietary guidelines for continued weight loss without complications.

That said, dozens of potential surgery clients opted out of the procedure. Working together, they found that they not only were successful at losing the 10% weight loss requirement but had also learned how to finally eat right. The result: they continued to lose weight without the surgery. I share a testimonial from one of my patients who, to this day, thanks me for finally teaching her how to eat right.

The thought of skipping a date with a scalpel and sitting down to a balanced 1:1:1 Meal was so reassuring to the thousands of people who have struggled with chronic dieting.

To know that I was able to change and shift the mindset of a patient who so desperately wanted to have surgery to someone who wanted to finally learn "HOW" to eat using the 1:1:1 Formula was quite rewarding.

Rawan Bin Hussain

I am from Kuwait

What I do: Legal adviser / Public Figure

Find me on:
- SnapChat: snpchat.com/add/rbinhussain

- YouTube:

youtube.com/channel/UC2uHK3nceP5RxjprZo5hxwg

- X: x.com/rbinhussain

I Get Up Quickly

Diverse Hobbies & Activities

I ENJOY HAVING DIVERSE hobbies and activities. These goals have nothing to do with work. They could be as simple as reading more or as ambitious as learning a new language. These goals enrich my life, help me develop new skills, and give me a sense of purpose outside my work.

I have always loved my culture, loved our food, and our cooking. While my university and work life kept me on planes and busy, the pandemic allowed me the time to explore this and become good at it. It is a feeling of accomplishment that I can't describe. This is why sometimes your personal goals don't exist in a vacuum. They have the potential to lead you towards a happier, more fulfilling career and lifestyle.

Exploring other creativity areas is the same as for me (it could be different for every individual). I spent time gardening, writing a journal every day, and staying consistent with a few activities that I knew I wanted to look into for a while now. Not only did it give me direction during some tough times, but it also set the pace for what I may like and what may interest me in the future.

I enjoy sharing my hobbies and trying out new activities with the people I love; it brings me a sense of fulfillment like no other.

Travel & Exploration

I've always loved traveling around the world, and it opens up so many doors; we meet new friends, are introduced to new cultures, and learn new languages. I feel grateful to have something more significant than anything with monetary value, all of this experience and insight. It is the vast network I have built around the globe over time. This network has allowed me to work with many international and local brands, which helped me grow professionally.

Every person I met has a story, and every word has a lesson I've learned, which helped me grow personally and mature. Sometimes, you have an individual perspective or view on life or a given culture, which can change, and it most probably will.

Result? Growth. New experiences stimulate your mind, allow you to learn new skills, and think differently about challenges and daily issues.

Travel has a unique way of exposing us to experiences that create a mental shift within us that you just can't find by any other means. I have learned that if we continue to seek unfamiliar surroundings, meet new people, and tackle uncertainty head-on, we will undoubtedly begin to notice a change within ourselves over time. An open mind will get you very far on your travels! It will help you remain receptive to change as you soak it all in, effectively stimulating inner growth along the way.

Additional Thoughts and Advice for Upcoming Entrepreneurs

I've learned that "what doesn't kill you makes you stronger." I've learned that I have no room for failure, and I've learned how to get up quickly after I fall. People go through adversity every day, whether it's the loss of a relationship or a person, stress at work or school, or just anything that may trouble someone's life. No matter what events you go through, you have the strength to do what you want.

I've learned to accept love and respect myself, my body, my features, and where I come from because it all makes me who I am today, unique and different from others. While everything in life comes with challenges, I have also realized that we have individual control and power over how we take these challenges.

While some pain and suffering in life are unavoidable and part of the human experience, much is self-induced by our thoughts and can be radically reduced by mindfulness practices and mental health tools. Learning to alter my thoughts has drastically improved my life. Working with the same types of challenges that used to cause me, such as panic, pain, and suffering, has provided me with a consistent level of calm, joy, optimism, and trust in myself and God's plan for me.

There are good people and bad ones, and we learn 'The Masters,' who teach us the lessons that we exist for and help us grow at all levels. I choose to believe that no one is bad.

Nobody is completely good or bad, but we sometimes select the wrong behaviors and prioritize our relationships' wrong feelings. Either way, bad experiences are a reality that we have to try to live with, or we should try to use them to learn lessons from life that help us return to our journey.

I don't think it is worth our time to remain in pain and obsess over what should have been. When a situation arises from a negative relationship or exchange, it causes us distress. Instead of making it bigger, I think we should train ourselves to take it as a learning experience.

I have learned to let go and that, not everything I desire or want is meant for me. God has bigger plans for us. Over time, I have learned to let myself go and allow life to take control, taking me in whatever direction is chosen for me and what is best for me. We must accept the person we are in this moment and how other people are.

As time goes on, we continue to learn that things don't always go as planned — actually, they pretty much never do.

And that's okay: If you become aware of yourself and your part of your relationships, they will improve; however, you may also have to accept facts about certain people in your life.

Practice gratitude, appreciation, and trust in the process.

Redwan Abudawood

I am from Jeddah, Saudi Arabia

What I do: I am a partner at Palm Ventures

Find me on:
- LinkedIn:

linkedin.com/in/redwan-abudawood-6a520b39
- X: x.com/redwanabudawood

Healthy Lifestyle and Habits Stem from Core Beliefs
About Life and Our Purpose

Healthy Lifestyle Habits

I CONSIDER MYSELF MODESTLY health-conscious. My 'awakening' story began in my freshman year at college when my biology professor at CU Boulder, Dr. Charlie Nuttelman, introduced me to the concept of a healthy lifestyle.

Dr Nuttelman introduced to me the concept of partially hydrogenated oils and how consuming these oils, which are still present in most junk food, is worse than smoking.

As life went on and I started to focus more on my big why and long-term objectives, I found myself in the company of like-minded, passionate, dear friends with whom I worked day and night on creating new projects and startups aiming to make an impact and accomplish financial independence.

That long-term vision and determination further fueled my journey toward better and healthier lifestyle habits.

As of this, it has been more than 9 years since I quit junk food and soft drinks and more than 5 years with almost no white rice, bread, or added sugar in my diet. I maintain 1-3 days of exercise weekly. Recently,

I have been practicing yoga almost daily. These habits are not merely to keep oneself in check but rather a godly obligation on our soles and bodies to embrace and serve our purpose in this life.

A healthy lifestyle and habits stem from core beliefs about life and our purpose. I highly suggest reading "7 Pillars of Health" by Dr. Don Colbert, which provides a well-balanced wellness overview and plan.

Regarding my daily routine and exercise schedule, I found that exercising works best for me either in the early morning before starting my work activities (which requires sleeping early) or late in the evening after rounding up my work schedule.

I would advise experimenting with your schedule to find what best works for you, but then selecting a specific time for practicing to make it stick.

Saleema Vellani

I am from Toronto / Reside in Washington, DC

What I do: Serial Entrepreneur

Find me on:
- My website: saleemavellani.com/thebook

- X: x.com/SaleemaVellani

- Facebook: facebook.com/saleemavellani

- Instagram: instagram.com/saleemavellani

- LinkedIn: linkedin.com/in/saleemavellani

Innovation Starts with Me

Self-Discovery & Improvement

SELF-DISCOVERY IS AN ONGOING part of life. With the world and technology moving at such a fast pace, we are being impacted daily, and as a result, we are constantly changing who we are.

During my first experience with a therapist, I was told that we are like onions. I was told that doing personal development work would help me peel layers to discover my true self and uncover my core values.

However, I found that there was only so much I could dig through before I hit a spiral of self-sabotage, where I always started seeking validation from others, and it took a toll on my confidence. I realized that I could peel only so many layers of the onion.

When my life crashed, and several events negatively impacted me over the course of a year, including getting laid off from all my gigs to being displaced for several months when my building had a destructive fire, it couldn't get any worse. To exacerbate the situation, I had trouble entering the United States when I returned from an Eat, Pray, Self-Love journey worldwide.

As a Canadian, I was given two weeks to find a job that would sponsor my visa. The hustle of setting up a 100 Coffee Challenge rebuilt my drive and resilience. It landed me a meaningful gig to research climate-smart solutions, such as hydroponics, to food insecurity for refugees in the Middle East and Africa.

Through reconnecting with my community, friends, and mentors, I realized how much people are willing to help when we simply ask. The new gig also led to many opportunities since I developed a real use case for social innovation that is still one of my favorite impact stories. It had a ripple effect.

I started teaching entrepreneurship and design thinking as I entered the design thinking and innovation fields. I became a keynote speaker and am now the author of Innovation Starts with Me, where I share my story.

I learned that we could peel our layers as we go through self-discovery, but we need to grow more layers simultaneously by doing impactful work aligned with our purpose and getting better at it over time. Our sweet spot is not just discovered; it's also developed.

I resonate with all of these, some more than others, at different phases of my journey.

Travel & exploration, continuous learning, and self-discovery & improvement have been the most critical constants.

Substantial spiritual depth has been significant during some of my most challenging times.

I am passionate about technology and tools and have a creative, open mindset, especially when it comes to business.

Regarding playing, I love taking on new hobbies and partaking in multiple activities, especially with my friends and community.

Additional Thoughts and Advice for Upcoming Entrepreneurs

Below is a tool I created to help you discover and develop your sweet spot.

Our life is like a series of projects. Try not to see your career as a series of jobs.

Take a flipchart, use a whiteboard, or even a piece of paper, and map out all the projects you've executed or contributed to. Which ones did you excel at the most? Which ones did you get the most positive feedback from? Which ones did you enjoy, and would you even do for free? Fill in these quadrants first and reflect on them.

What are some ideas you've had in mind that are likely out of your comfort zone that you've considered experimenting with? For example, have you thought of starting a blog or podcast? Have you wanted to write a book or do more public speaking?

If they don't readily come to mind, or if you don't have any specific ones on the back burner, then ask a few of your friends and colleagues what types of projects or activities they think of when they think of you.

If you're comfortable with it, share the three filled-out quadrants to give them some context regarding what you've already done in a snapshot.

Your sweet spot will likely be discovered and developed as you work on those new projects.

EXCELLED AT
Which projects did you excel at?
You're confident in these skills and others know you have them too.

PRAISED FOR
Which projects did you receive the most positive feedback on?
Some of the praise may have surprised you

Finding Your **Sweet Spot**

LOVED DOING
Which projects gave you the most joy?
Think about the projects that you felt most passionate about.

OPEN TO TESTING
Which projects have you been keeping on the backburner?
These are projects that are outside of your comfort zone that you're willing to test

SALEEMA VELLANI ©

Stefan Avivson

I am from Aarhus, Denmark

What I do:
CEO & Founder of BMoreRaw.com.
I'm a serial entrepreneur and rock musician.
My lifestyle is living life. I see no difference between business and free time. I believe everything you do must be done with pleasure, so why not make it so?

Find me on:
- LinkedIn: linkedin.com/in/avivso/

A Life Mission Will Keep You Going

Strong Spiritual Depth

EIGHT YEARS AGO, I had a unicorn in the shipping industry. With the software we created at that time, we changed the world and the way people work in the industry. Unfortunately, our investor died. At that time, I learned that you could not raise more money with a dead investment law.

That's pretty hard. So, I spent all my money trying to save the company, but I didn't. So, I lost all my money, my mother died, and literally, my entire life changed. I used to be a millionaire running around, flying around, having fun, and suddenly, with no money, yeah, you're not roaming, stuck in one place.

Due to those things, I had depression for three years. I went on the discovery, trying to find out what would make me happy, and I learned that what makes me happy is to help other people. If I help other people, it makes me happy. I don't care if you're having fun if you follow me in that sense. Having a goal in your life changes your attitude completely towards actually living life instead of hunting life.

So, what I believe you should do, especially as an entrepreneur, is find your mission in life. The mission in life is typically much more extensive than what a company can deliver. Still, you have something to achieve as long as you have a mission when you have something to achieve that also offers some other cool things as people keep involved with what you believe is essential in life.

When that is present, you avoid the only proper thing that kills people besides diseases and loneliness. So, what I learned in my spiritual way is that I need to understand my mission in life so I have a higher goal, so I know what I'm doing, and so I can always put whatever I do into that context.

Diverse Hobbies & Activities

You need to find something fun that makes you happy. Something you can focus your mind on that isn't your start-up. If you are a real entrepreneur, you spend 100% of your time thinking about your startup, even when you sleep.

But, when you think of the same things all the way through, you're unable to reflect.

Reflection is a very, very important part of reaching a higher step and wanting something more significant. So, find a hobby and stick to it to help you get your mind off your business for a while.

Healthy Lifestyle Habits

One thing that has helped me a lot is adopting a healthy lifestyle. I used to weigh 130 kilos but lost 50, which gave me more energy. I just skipped wheat, meat, and alcohol.

Tejinder Singh

I am from India

What I do: Entrepreneur, Digital Nomad, Startups Investor

Find me on:
- LinkedIn: linkedin.com/in/teji05

What Change Can You Bring?

Ideation & Creation

IDEATION AND CREATION HAVE been the essential pillar and foundation of my thought process my entire life. I have been a creative and ideation guy since the beginning. I have always been in love with creativity as it's the only thing that, to me, is original. Be it a logo or the startups I have created throughout my life, I have always worked on the blue ocean.

Creativity always gives you originality. I have started over 20 startups and exited almost 5; the key to this has always been original ideation.

Therefore, this is the essential pillar of everything I have done and continue to do.

I marshaled the ideation and growth of Sparsh, the first-ever onshore BPO for India. It was the first to be listed on the stock market and the first to be acquired in the domestic BPO space (by Blackstone-backed Intelenet Global Inc.).

I took the growth of Sparsh from ZERO to 8500+ team size in less than three years across five cities of India, serving telecom, retail, Airlines, BFSI, and many more verticals; Intelenet, backed by Blackstone, later acquired it.

Always think about what change you can bring. What is the problem which doesn't have a solution? Why hasn't there been an answer until now? What were the reasons for it?

If you think through all these, you will most likely give birth to an idea that will be creative enough to be unique and perhaps commercially successful.

Timi Orija

I am from London, United Kingdom

What I do: CEO at 4s-Events

Find me on:
- Instagram: instagram.com/4seventslondon

- My website: https://4s-events.com

Be Sure to Follow Your Dreams and Passion

Self-Discovery & Improvement

I WENT FROM DROPPING out and not finishing my degree in Management and Marketing to running a bespoke lifestyle management company.

We look after client requests from a global clientele. We source art, real estate, b2b introductions, and tickets to invitation-only events.

Furthermore, I was headhunted to manage the PR and marketing of a young, exciting racing driver, Ayrton Simmons.

We cover everything from talking to brands and sponsorship opportunities to learning about the mind and sports psychology conditioning. Things are constantly evolving, both personally and professionally.

Much of this was created from the mindset of helping others.

An example is raising awareness and sponsorship for the team. It is not a 9-to-5 role, so being innovative and thinking outside the box is key to bringing success off the track.

This interview is an example.

Additional Thoughts and Advice for Upcoming Entrepreneurs

Never be afraid to learn the hard way and get stuck in a task or a role. This is part of the growth process.

Always learn and try. If it fails, it's not the end of the world. Try again and fail better the next time.

Always read and keep up to date on current affairs. This could have a knock-on effect on your industry. The lack of traveling and tourism in the country is an example. The lack of hotel, restaurant, and store guests has affected the balance sheets of many well-established businesses.

Learn to give as much as you receive. The good guys can also win too, although it might take longer. There are no such things as shortcuts in life or business.

Peace of mind is a beautiful thing.

Follow your dreams and passion. No one's time is promised here on earth, and we could be gone tomorrow. Start today. Today is the first day of the rest of your life.

Vasiliy Ivanov

I am from Ukraine

What I do: Founder of KeepSolid

Find me on:
- LinkedIn: linkedin.com/in/vasiliyivanov/

- X: x.com/vasyl_keepsolid

No Person Is Less Rational Than the One Who Thinks, "I Know Everything"

Ideation & Creation

SINCE I WAS YOUNG, I have enjoyed creating to avoid boredom. When I got my first PC, it opened up incredible opportunities for me. I got excited and began my attempts to create something using the computer—from design to programming to hardware. The passion for creating something new stayed with me even after I got a job.

THE FLOURISHING ENTREPRENEURIAL LIFESTYLE

I kept experimenting, trying my hand at making all sorts of software products. This is how my first startups and, eventually, KeepSolid were born.

An important thing here was to learn to manage resources properly and not take on everything at once. At one point, I flushed my entire budget down the drain by trying to run many projects simultaneously. Out of 6 products, we finished 2, and only one succeeded.

Self-Discovery & Improvement

No person is less rational than the one who thinks, "I know everything." I was like that. Then, a person appeared in my life who helped me see that all my opinions about the causes of problems are just my point of view, not reality.

Since then, I have looked at the world and people differently. I realized that different people perceive reality differently, even when discussing the same mug. This realization dramatically changed my attitude towards people and showed how much there is still to develop in my personality.

Using the Right Tools

As the head of an IT company, I realize how many opportunities modern technologies give us. A computer can now complete tasks in mere seconds that would previously take dozens of people. Where possible, I try to teach friends and colleagues about how to use technology more effectively.

When hiking, I always used a map and compass to navigate. It was not easy to arrive at the right place on Ime. Nowadays, digital maps certainly simplify this process.

They can even calculate travel times while taking into account stuff like traffic jams.

Fantastic!

On the other hand, I see how dangerous these tools can be for the human mind. The longer we interact with the computer, the less sociable and friendly we become. Just look at young people in countries where children have mobile phones from an early age; this is a new form of addiction.

People glance away from their phones, and this world seems hostile to them, so they dive into their phones again. The situation can negatively affect the next generation. That's why I always encourage my friends to distract children from their phones and do something real.

Healthy Lifestyle Habits

At first, we have no time for sports because we are busy with work, and then we have no time for work because our bodies start falling apart. I realized this after a long break in sports and felt all the buzz of physical exercise again.

Open & Balanced Mindset

While looking for mistakes in others, I had no chance to fix any situation. I was surprised to learn that I am the cause of everything that happens around me. With it, I acquired a superpower - the ability to overcome any problem :)

Continuous Learning

Recently, I have formulated an idea of development for my employees: personal development is not an increase in knowledge in some area but an increase in abilities.

For example, a programmer may know five programming languages and 20 technologies but still write low-quality code. A programmer who knows only one programming language but has learned to do it efficiently will make their manager much more satisfied with the results.

Travel & Exploration

When my wife and I began to travel and get acquainted with different cultures, we realized how little we knew about the world. Learning about other nations' history, ways of thinking, and life principles is exciting. This knowledge proved useful for the business, too. I realized that our customers in different parts of the world think entirely differently and have different product expectations.

Following Latest Technologies

One of the most painful situations for a businessman is to find out that someone else has already implemented your idea. It was like that for me when I would miss a modern trend.

Strong spiritual depth

A few years ago, I was lucky to figure out wisdom: there are no bad people, but there are many negative experiences. An experience that prevents them from acting with good intentions. It became an essential principle of my behavior - in addition to finding good people/employees, I decided to help those who were already with me to overcome their issues.

Hobbies & Activities

I am lucky to have friends with whom I can share various hobbies—sports, driving, travel, etc. Most importantly, having the right hobbies can help you take your mind off problems or difficult tasks. When completely immersed in a hobby, all my attention switches to what I'm doing. It provides both a rest for the mind and an opportunity to find a solution when I return to work.

A person's development is determined by their desire to create something in various areas of life. These ten pillars are a great way to build a detailed personal development plan. I would be happy to see such a plan to motivate children since school!

Viviane Paraschiv

I am Romanian born in Belgium, living between London and Brussels

What I do: Working full time at Farfetch and co-founder of Twist Supper Club

Find me on:
- Instagram: instagram.com/thisisvivp

- LinkedIn: linkedin.com/in/vivianeparaschiv

It's a Marathon with People Sometimes Throwing Bananas at You

Self-Discovery and Improvement

IT'S ALMOST BREATHTAKING TO think about how much I've developed personally since starting to work more than ten years ago. Many people talk about the importance of self-improvement but fail to recognize that it's something you must do gradually and regularly. This can hurt since not everyone is good at giving feedback.

You often hear that "it's a marathon," but I want to add, "It's a marathon with people sometimes throwing bananas at you, and what matters is what you do with the banana."

When I started my professional life, I thought I had to hide my bubbly and outgoing personality; otherwise, people wouldn't take me seriously. So, from the first day in my new role, I was laser-focused, making sure I was making a good impression, telling off my colleagues who were not following the rules, and trying to stand out in individual meetings or situations to show how smart I was. That all came from self-doubt and wanting to prove something to others.;

I was successful in getting up the ranks quite quickly. Still, it also obviously backfired after a while, with people in my team thinking I was backstabbing them (when I am a very loyal person) or saying I was only fun for 30 minutes a day. It was excruciating to hear because I never wanted my colleagues to think I was doing well.

After the initial reaction, I took some time to reflect on it, thinking about what led to the current situation and how I could improve. You have the power to change any problem if you are willing to change your approach and the angle you're looking at it from because receiving negative feedback doesn't mean you've failed. Still, it's an opportunity to go further on your journey of self-discovery and improvement.

Always ask for feedback, even if you are uncomfortable or think someone might not give you positive feedback. Once a week (usually on Friday), take a few minutes to reflect and provide feedback on the past few days. Also, acknowledge someone you worked with through a little message, a short email, a quick note, or a word in the elevator. Give some to get some back later!

Also, listen to Audible to Brenee Brown's audiobook "The Power of Vulnerability." It's brilliant!

If you only have 20 minutes, listen to her various TED Talks. That woman is not only smart but also very funny.

Continuous Learning

We often hear how important it is to learn at school and university with society, our parents, and everyone putting pressure on those "formative years." But what I've realized is that learning never stops, or it should never stop.

I have an inquisitive personality, so I'm attracted to newness and the unknown. This makes continuous learning easy, and I see this quality as more important as we progress in this unfamiliar world.

Being a professional in Change Management and having led entire retail teams on Retail Transformation at Ralph Lauren, for example,

I have seen firsthand how some of my staff and colleagues embraced new tools and ways of working more quickly than others. It wasn't a matter of age, education, or other criteria. It was their mindset and the way they embraced change.

You can acquire and develop continuous learning over time, but it's not instant if you've never been taught to think that way. Adopting new situations and learning new skills, techniques, tools, and technology is crucial to survival and staying relevant.

Try following or subscribing to one newsletter or magazine outside your comfort zone or expertise. I assure you that you will always learn something new and probably even spark some ideas for your job/project/current situation.

If you haven't heard about it yet, read about the "Growth Mindset." One of my favorites is the Ted Talk with Carol Dweck[1].

Using the Right Tools

I am a bit obsessed with the idea of using the correct tools because you can lose a lot of valuable time if you do not support your objectives.

When I was working at Louis Vuitton, we spent hours putting together a document that had to be read by our senior directors before important events. Hence, it was a very stressful exercise. We were compiling the information. Building this document was all very manual, usually updated until the last minute, and involved a lot of copying and pasting, leading to many possible errors and nightmares.

While we were stuck in the wheel like little rats in a lab, I realized there could be a better way of doing this. Unfortunately, I left the role a few months later and never got the chance to implement my findings.

However, when I shared these insights with my previous manager, who was still in that role, she said it was a game-changer and could free up time for the team to focus on more critical tasks and stop having sleepless nights about this crazy document!

It shows you that using the right tool is just as important as the rest. You should always ensure it answers your needs and know that no device is perfect.

---

1. https://www.ted.com/talks/carol_dweck_the_power_of_belie ving_that_you_can_improve%3Flanguage%3Den

Yousef Hammoda

I am from Syria and living in UAE

What I do: Entrepreneur, Marketing Wizard & Global Citizen

Find me on:
- My website: www.hammoda.com

- LinkedIn: linkedin.com/in/yousefhammoda

- X: x.com/yousef_hammoda

- Instagram: instagram.com/yousef.hammoda

We Need to Be Open and Ready to Learn

Self-Discovery & Improvement

WE ARE BORN EQUIPPED with some skills, but many of us don't know what those skills we already have; here, self-discovery gets started, so we need to discover what we call then improve it so we can get the best out of it, everyone is different by the way.

I realized I was excellent at people communication and could always break the ice, so I started working in media and advertising, mainly about communications.

Later, I realized I'm useful in managing people and keeping a happy environment.

Knowing my strengths means I endeavor to boost the team's performance and get the best out of everyone.

Using the Right Tools

We need to know the available tools to use the right tools. It's always a new learning process. For example, I used ASANA to manage the team task in project management. My project manager told me about Jira, so I was open to learning and implementing a better way to manage the team task.

So, it's always about what you do and how ready you and your team are to use a new tool to improve the work. But tools will save you a lot of time if you know how to use them; I suggest asking an expert or trying to keep yourself updated and always being open to learning.

Continuous Learning

I could talk a lot about this topic, but I will try to be brief as much as possible to get the idea.

As I mentioned earlier, when using the tools, we need to be open and ready to learn, not only about the tools but also about many things in our lives.

Learning allows us to make better decisions and actions in our lives. If you are in a business, that will help you manage the team even more. I started learning about computer networking, servers, and programming languages, which helped me start my first job and later start my first business.

Then, I learned more about colors and branding, using digital media, running ads on Google and social media, and how to target the right audience. Because I needed to manage a team, I learned how to maintain a happy working environment. As an entrepreneur, you will be forced to keep learning new things as you work on multiple business segments.

Strong Spiritual Depth

It's the belief that what you do today will be great tomorrow. Believe that God will always be there for you as he has been there all those years. Be thankful for what you do, always look for more, be hungry to achieve, and have great faith that tomorrow will always be better.

Yousuf Aqeel

I am from Perth, Australia

What I do: CEO of Fidelity Digital (Marketing and Media Agency)

Find me on:
- LinkedIn: linkedin.com/in/yousuf-aqeel-41897536

Stay Away from Things That Don't Produce Results

Continuous Learning

THE MORE YOU GAIN knowledge and grow as a professional and a person, the better equipped you will be to impact the people around you.

I have learned that associating with the right person or people in your life can help you propel yourself to the next phase. Learning from other people, their mistakes and their experiences cut down my learning curve and the years I could have spent learning something through my own experience.

I was born in Pakistan and spent my early schooling and childhood there until I was 17. Then, I went to England to study for my undergraduate degree. So, as you know, that's where my journey began, pretty much when I started living independently.

My life experience has shown me that the more you learn, the more you earn. The more you understand your surroundings, the more your capabilities increase. You also tend to avoid things that don't work for you, which, in turn, will lead to exponential growth in your business.

Also, learn from your mistakes and, again, stay away from things that do not produce results that don't give you some satisfaction or translate to your life goals. Further, learning from experiences is also powerful. It means that as you inevitably encounter mistakes throughout your journey, you become wiser and better since you're less likely to repeat those same mistakes.

I aim to be location-independent and financially confident so I can work from anywhere, wherever, and however I want.

I tried many different online business ventures. I sold products on Amazon and built my website—an e-commerce platform where we sold kitchen gadgets and more. Most of those businesses demanded a lot of local marketing, which I started to do. I would build landing pages, set up Facebook ads, and handle other aspects of digital marketing.

I worked with suppliers and manufacturers worldwide and pursued 8 to 10 other business ideas. Some worked, some failed.

I had an amazing experience, and I figured out what I was good at: talking to people, solving their problems, and really understanding their business. With time, I focused on marketing consultancy, and that's how my marketing and media agency, Fidelity Digital, was born.

Thoughts on Growth

Blog Reflections From The FELS Lifestyle

THIS SECTION SHOWS VARIOUS samplings of our blog posts in several languages across our global social media network. As you'll notice, we typically use our special "content frame" in post designs, with an icon at the bottom left to denote which FELS pillar is in focus.

I invite you to check our blog posts on https://myfels.com/#feed.

The posts in this chapter cover all ten pillars, offering clear examples of how they are embodied and practiced. You can also access our full blog online at any time at https://my-fels.life/posts/.

(Please note that some posts contain linked articles and images from the Internet for social media sharing. They are displayed here only for ease of reference and do not constitute part of the book, and we do not claim copyright to them as they belong to their original publishers.)

Book Recommendation: Genius Food

Can certain foods make you smarter and more productive?

According to research by famous documentarian Max Lugavere and his co-author, Dr Paul Grewal, the answer is yes.

Powerful superfoods, such as almonds, wild salmon, grass-fed beef, blueberries, and olive oil, can boost and protect our brains while helping improve our mood and focus.

Grab this book to learn which genius foods to stock up on and the ideal ways to consume them.

Tanzania, Asante!

With only around 500 cases identified so far, Tanzania is fortunate to be one of the least affected countries by the coronavirus pandemic. After things settle, it will surely be a top destination for travelers, with its quaint capital city of Dar-es-Salam and pristine clear-blue beaches off the coast of Zanzibar.

Visitors can easily learn simple phrases of the local Swahili language, like "Asante" (thank you) and the famous "Hakuna

Matata" (no worries) popularized by Disney's Lion King Productions—even the name "Simba" means lion in their language!

Robots Help Out During The Pandemic

This dog-shaped Spot robot by Boston Dynamics has been busy assisting humanity in various ways during the current global pandemic.

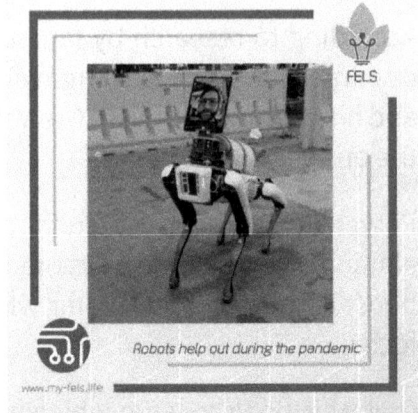

Robots help out during the pandemic

For example, Singapore uses it to help enforce social distancing rules between people outside. In other places, hospitals use it to reduce the direct contact healthcare workers must have with patients (see the full article and videos on *Popular Mechanics* at https://bit.ly/2TCe7ye).

Where do you think the field of robotics is heading in the near future, and where else do you think they can come to our help?

Book Recommendation: Peak Performance by Steve & Brad

In this insightful book, authors Steve Magness and Brad Stulberg show from personal experience how extraordinary performance can often lead to burnout and stagnation. Then, they teach us how to turn that around and turn it into sustainable long-term success and happiness instead. Learn how to strive for your dreams correctly without losing track or purpose by understanding the science behind elevating and optimizing human performance in any pursuit.

How Many Languages Do You Speak?

Languages are quite interesting, like an operating system for humans. They carry all the words and expressions that bring meaning to all facets of life around us and teach us how to think and explore the world in certain ways. If you learn multiple languages (even just a bit of each), you'll have the pleasure of seeing how each linguistic culture views the world through its symbolism, metaphors, and poetic expression. Try learning a new language these days so you'll be ready when traveling opens up later on – to get a nice tour of languages and which ones could be preferable to you phonetically or easy to learn, check out the amazing collection of videos by Paul on the LangFocus channel.

System Sounds: A New Perspective on The Universe

Want to expand your mental horizons? Look at this inspirational TED Talk by astrophysicist/musician Matt Russo, who dazzles us by transforming physical planetary movements into harmonious musical sounds, thus showing our universe in an exciting new way. Treat your mind to this audiovisual odyssey and see how blending disciplines such as science, art, and music can lead to new concepts and perspectives.

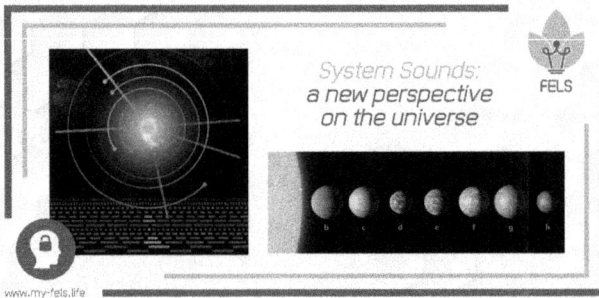

Try the Keto Diet!

You have probably been hearing the word "keto" or the ketogenic lifestyle in general lately as it has been buzzing around the world and catching attention. Its basic theory is that our bodies can run mostly on fat metabolites (ketones) as a cleaner fuel than the carb-based diet we tend to have normally. Followers of this lifestyle typically get around 70% of their caloric intake from healthy fats, 25% from protein, and the remaining tiny portion from carbs. These abundant fats include oils

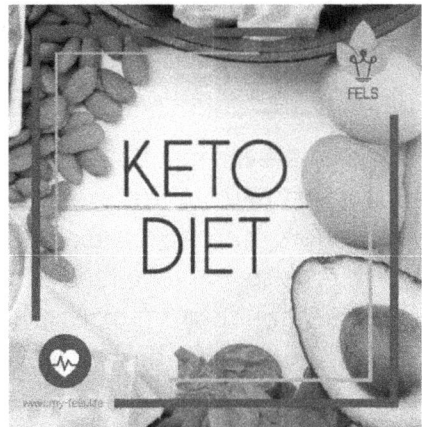

of avocado, coconut, olive, nuts, fish, and organic or grass-fed dairy butter.

Pick up a guide or app that can help you through this eating style and reap some of the commonly reported benefits, such as improved mood and focus, better sleep, boosted immunity, and sustained weight loss.

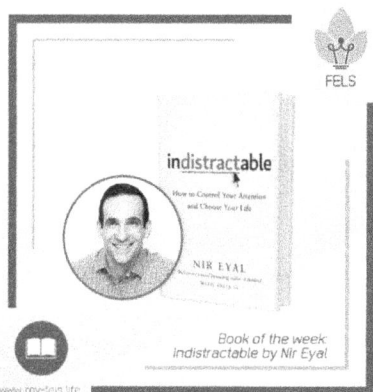

Book of the week:
indistractable by Nir Eyal

Book Recommendation: Indistractable by Nir Eyal

While many of us are getting used to working from home lately, it becomes important to learn how to stay focused on the tasks at hand and not be constantly swayed by diversions and distractions. This insightful book by famous writer and psychologist Nir Eyal offers practical tips on making yourself "Indistractable" whether for work or in relationships and family interactions. It also talks about keeping children away from modern-day distractions in our world filled with flashy gadgets and endless online content.

Have You Tried Meditation?

You may have heard a lot about meditation, mindfulness, and related exercises like yoga and tai chi. Several recent studies have proven that meditation has tangible benefits, such as calming the mind and reducing stress, improving self-awareness and balance, and sharpening one's sense of empathy and connectedness with others. Take this time of solitude to try some of these practices using the numerous guides and apps available to get you started easily.

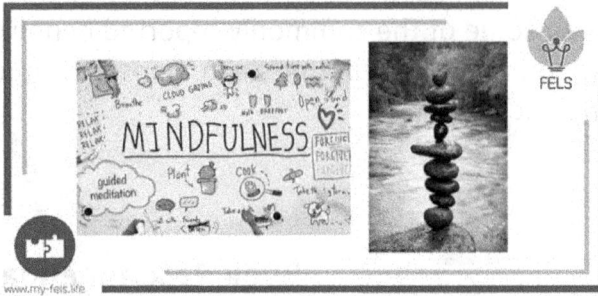

Song of Ambition: Proud

What have you done today to make you feel proud?

UK singer Heather Small poses this question of encouragement in her song "The Anthem," originally released in 2000 and used again as the official anthem for the London Olympics in 2012. Listen and challenge yourself always to have at least one daily achievement that gives you a sense of elevation and growth, even if just a small measure!

https://www.youtube.com/watch?v=LEoxGJ79PMs

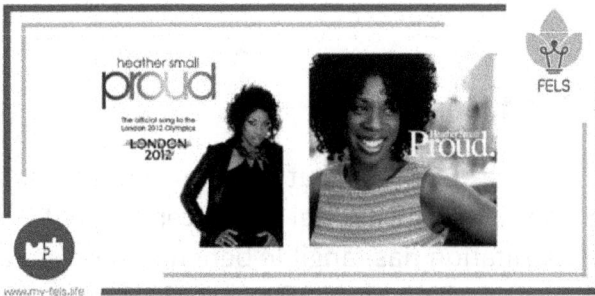

Eat More Fish!

As you may have seen in one of our previous posts, the key supplements for a strong immune system include vitamins A, C, D, and Omega-3 essential fats. So, if you don't enjoy taking too many pills, is there food in nature that has most of these naturally?

Eat More Fish!

Yes, fish! Most fish are tasty and healthy, though cold-water fatty fish—such as wild salmon, mackerel, and sardines—are especially rich in these nutrients. Try to get these around 2-3 times each week or on any possible occasion. Have them alone or in a salad or soup… any way you prefer, you'll get the benefits and keep fighting off potential illnesses.

Skills & Preferences Inventory

When was the last time you sat down and thought about the things you are good at and enjoy doing? The current downturn period might be a great chance for some thorough introspective analysis, looking inside yourself to identify your top skills and preferences for work and other areas of life. If your current field of work doesn't match your attributes & interests well, it might be time to research a career or business change. It's always worth pursuing something you have a talent and passion for, and the rewards will follow naturally! Many tools & tests are available online to help you do a good self-assessment & discovery exercise, so this is a recommended use of your time in isolation.

Online Business Always Prevails

I have always been a proponent of online businesses, recommending them to people through my entrepreneurship consulting practice. As we can see now, there are very good reasons for that! Besides being less costly and risky to start than traditional ones, online businesses can survive most calamities, as we are witnessing today.

While physical business outlets have shut their doors and lost income, online activities have prevailed and risen to the occasion, such as apps (think delivery and ride-sharing) and web technologies (distance learning, video calling, and the like). Technology never sleeps! My advice to aspiring entrepreneurs will always be to think online, not physically.

Eat Well, Sleep Well, and Stay Well These Days!

During this period, people in many countries were confined to their homes, so it was important to maintain a healthy diet and good sleeping habits, especially since there were limited options for mobility and exercise.

It was unfortunate to see many people stocking up on snack chips and sweetened cereals, which carry a high carb load and would only cause ongoing cravings to eat even more. This period could be a perfect time to practice some intermittent fasting and lower calorie intake since there are mostly no dinner parties or events to derail our diets as they usually do, and also less stress from working hours or travel, which may cause erratic eating habits. Use the isolation period wisely and isolate yourself from bad foods!

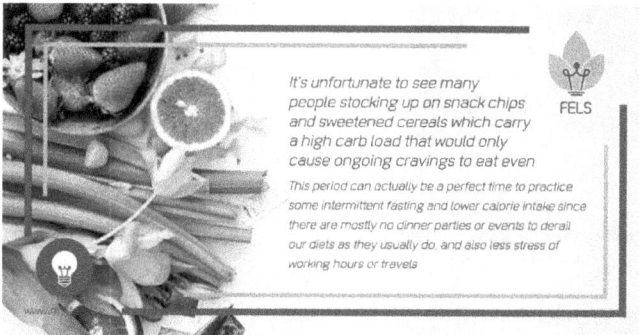

It's unfortunate to see many people stocking up on snack chips and sweetened cereals which carry a high carb load that would only cause ongoing cravings to eat even

This period can actually be a perfect time to practice some intermittent fasting and lower calorie intake since there are mostly no dinner parties or events to derail our diets as they usually do, and also less stress of working hours or travels

FELS

Healthy or Not? Quinoa Salad

Great combination of quinoa grains, leafy green vegetables, fresh avocado, and half-cooked egg.

What do you think?

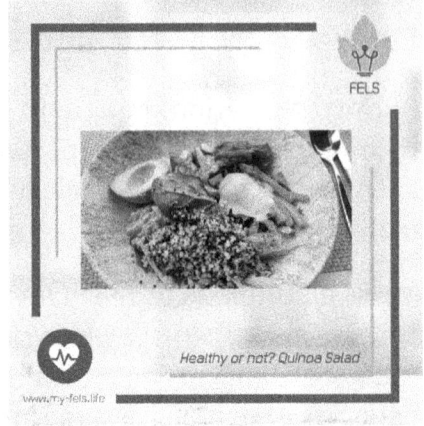

Healthy or not? Quinoa Salad
www.my-fels.life

The COVID-19 outbreak will boost the use of robotic cars
www.my-fels.life

The Pandemic Boosts The Use of Robotic Cars

Self-driving cars have been developed over the last decade by companies like @Tesla and others, but the wake has recently slowed down with slow adoption. With this virus outbreak, however, this technology is quickly resurging as people worldwide try to find ways to perform transportation services (such as ride-hailing or food and medicine delivery) while limiting human contact.

This outbreak has shown us that robotic cars are indeed useful, more as a necessity than a luxury. In addition to reducing road accidents and optimizing traffic, these vehicles can also help humans separated by quarantine or any similar natural disaster—may God forbid.

Song of Ambition: Am I Wrong?

Would you be wrong to have ambitions and dreams bigger than those around you? Is it bad to stretch yourself and reach for the stars?

Norwegian artists Nico and Vinz musically present these interesting questions in their popular 2013 song. Listen, and remember to always pursue your huge goals and visions, no matter what anyone says!

FELS

Song of Ambition: Am I Wrong?

www.my-fels.life

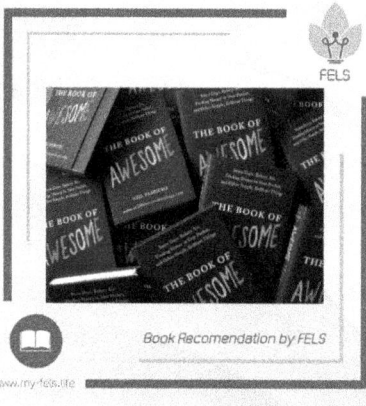

FELS

Book Recomendation by FELS

www.my-fels.life

The Book of Awesome: Small Things to Make You Feel Good

This cute little book by Neil Pasricha enlightens us on how to notice, savor, and enjoy the little pleasures in life, which can help us disconnect from daily stress and anxiety. In this much-needed time, the book is a heart-warming read that will surely get our minds off world problems and focus on tiny comforts we can find in our homes or anywhere around us.

Base Jumping

This fun activity is guaranteed to push you out of your comfort zone and give you an invigorating thrill! Look for a place near you that offers a safe high-jumping experience, then dare yourself to step off the edge and free-fall to the bottom.

Base Jumping

This picture is from Auckland Tower (NZ), over 300m tall.

The Deal with Energy Bars

Everyone seems crazy about energy bars lately, and you find a huge section for them in most supermarkets or health stores. So what's the deal? Most bars tend to be loaded with carbs (cereal pieces and sugary fruits) and should be avoided. Low-sugar bars can be quite healthy but hard to find. The brands shown here from our collection are awesome, and any bar labeled as "keto-friendly" or similar is guaranteed to have low sugar while offering a good amount of protein, fiber, and healthy fats.

The Deal with Energy Bars

Computer Games Can Actually Be Good For You!

With many people stuck indoors during these coming weeks, it can be a refreshing experience to download and play some interesting video or computer games.

Recent research has shown that playing moderate (preferably non-violent) games can increase mental sharpness and alertness while developing problem-solving and reaction skills. With the exclusion of highly simplified mobile games, mainly designed to pass the time, games made for computers or consoles often feature elaborate productions with intriguing stories, music, visuals, and the social aspect of playing with an online community.

Use this unplanned downtime to try new games in any area of interest and spend some time in a fun alternative to the real one!

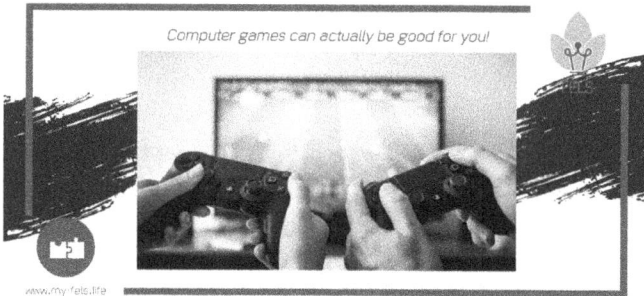

Computer games can actually be good for you!

www.my-fels.life

Do You Really Want It? Gotta Go and Get It!

In 1994, this song went "viral" along with Ricky Martin's electrifying stage performance. Combining catchy English, Spanish, and French lyrics, the song appealed to a wide global audience during the summer World Cup season. To this day, it remains an inspiring motivational song that can lift spirits and energize people to pursue what they really want and go after it with everything they have!

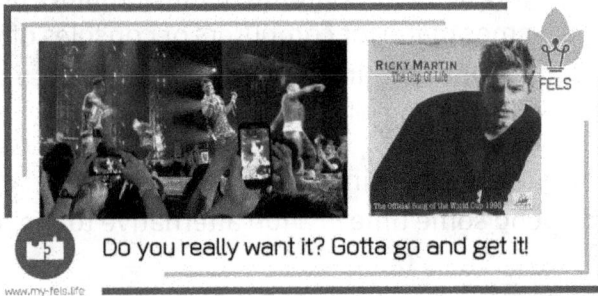

Do you really want it? Gotta go and get it!

www.my-fels.life

Food on a hot plate

www.my-fels.life

Food on a Hot Plate

Some Asian restaurant chains (such as Pepper Lunch) serve this concept: The meal is presented raw on a sizzling hot plate, and you decide how much to cook it. It features healthy components such as meat, vegetables, and eggs with few carbohydrates.

Book Recommendation: Game Changers by Dave Asprey

This interesting book, by the renowned biohacker and creator of the Bulletproof Diet, presents optimal lifestyle habits. It culls the wisdom of world-class thought leaders, maverick scientists, and disruptive entrepreneurs to provide proven techniques for becoming happier, healthier, and smarter.

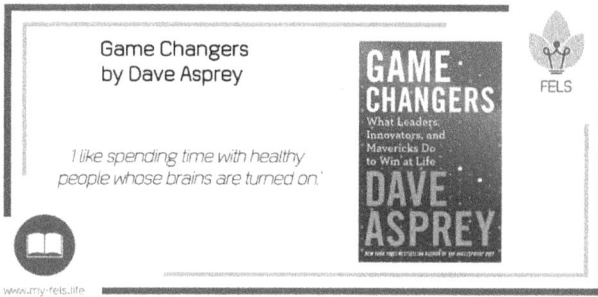

Game Changers
by Dave Asprey

'I like spending time with healthy people whose brains are turned on.'

GAME CHANGERS
What Leaders, Innovators, and Mavericks Do to Win at Life

DAVE ASPREY

FELS

www.my-fels.life

Genting Highlands: Entertainment Above the Clouds

This huge, modern complex is located atop a mountain peak in Malaysia. It offers countless options for shopping, dining, and entertainment.

Comment with your experience if you've been there!

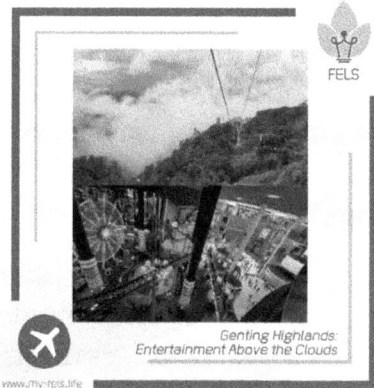

Genting Highlands:
Entertainment Above the Clouds

FELS

www.my-fels.life

Space Exploration
www.my-fels.life

Space Exploration

Until now, space probes have been able to land and photograph at least four large objects in the solar system: Venus, Mars, our moon, and Titan (a moon of Saturn).

So what do you think, so they all look similar?

Which place do you think will be, or should be next?

Which planet or place would you wish to visit sometime?

The Modern-day Constantinople

Istanbul, the city at the crossroads of Asia & Europe, has come a long way since the Ottoman Turks captured it in 1453.

The Modern-day Constantinople
www.my-fels.life

The beautiful Bosphorus shores are now lined with modern skyscrapers and business centers. However, the ancient Galata Tower still stands as a testament to its history as a Genovese trading post.

A new Netflix mini-series tells the amazing story of the siege and takeover of this majestic city. It is recommended for history buffs.

New Gadgets: Samsung Galaxy Z Flip

Released earlier this month, this innovative design solves the common problem of carrying a large smartphone in a small pocket. It looks great! Has anyone tried it? Let us know what you think and how durable and useful it is.

New Gadgets: #Samsung Galaxy Z Flip

Book Recommendation: Contagious by Jonah Berger

This book outlines the power of word-of-mouth and the six basic principles that drive things to become popular or viral. It is for everyone, whether you are a small business owner trying to boost awareness or a manager at a big company.

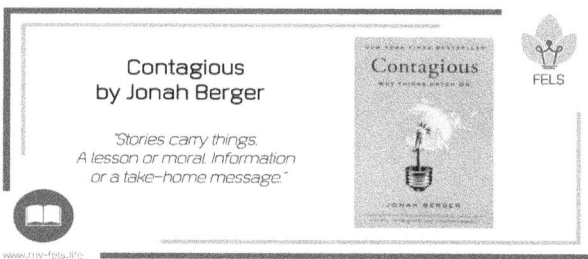

Contagious
by Jonah Berger

"Stories carry things.
A lesson or moral. Information
or a take-home message."

Tropical Fruits

Brazil is known for its fresh and juicy coconuts, a very healthy source of fat, making refreshing cold drinks from the milky water inside. Brazil is also famous for another popular and nutrient-rich superfood: acai berries.

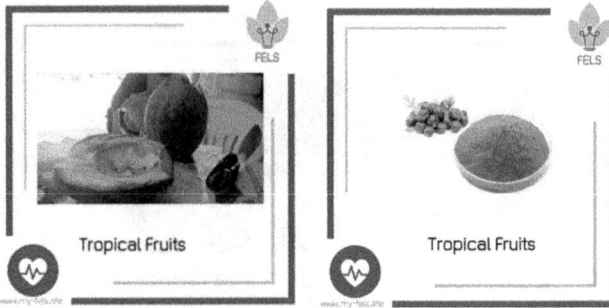

Tropical Fruits

Tropical Fruits

Anyone Been to Kyrgyzstan?

Full of culture and history, this country is an inexpensive destination for adventure travel and discovery. The capital city of Bishkek is surrounded by rugged mountains and lakes ready for exploration.

Try having a huge eagle staring you close in the eyes within biting distance for an added thrill!

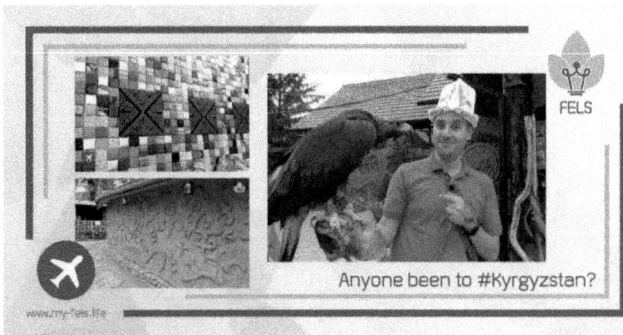

Anyone been to #Kyrgyzstan?

Carnival in Brazil

It is that time of year when the streets of Rio de Janeiro gather two million people daily to celebrate its annual festival. The Carnival in Rio, also known as "the biggest show on Earth," has massive and elaborate productions, with costumes and props costing around $250 million. Though most of the action occurs on the streets and block parties, these photos are from the official parade inside a huge, purpose-built stadium (the Sambodromo). The parade lasts all night for several consecutive days.

These are throwback pictures from the 2010 Carnival. Video link: https://youtu.be/hQs58CQ-AHU

Superfood Salads

Salmon and avocado contain all the good fats, and the fish protein and fiber from beans will help keep you full longer. Try superfood salad recipes with added berries, nuts, and eggs (skip the breadstick!).

What's The Deal With Tandoori Chicken?

Not commenting on Indian food here, but this dish with the famous oven-roasted chicken can be healthy as long as we don't eat too much of that tasty garlic bread on the side!

FELS

Abu Dhabi – A Rising Star of Business & Culture

The UAE's famous capital city has quietly become a hotspot for arts, entertainment, and tech businesses. Abu Dhabi Global attracts tourists with iconic venues such as Ferrari World and the Louvre Museum.

It also attracts startup entrepreneurs with various top incubator and accelerator programs, such as TwoFour54 (for media), Flat6 Labs (for tech), and StartAD, part of the New York University campus.

Book Recommendation: BEHAVE, by Robert Sapolsky

This book provides deep insights into human behavior at its best and worst while shedding light on the biological background of our range of behaviors and how they evolved. It is useful reading for anyone wishing to understand better and deal with humans!

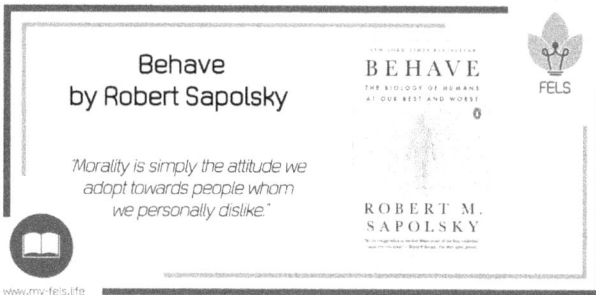

Behave
by Robert Sapolsky

"Morality is simply the attitude we adopt towards people whom we personally dislike."

BEHAVE
THE BIOLOGY OF HUMANS
AT OUR BEST AND WORST

FELS

ROBERT M. SAPOLSKY

www.my-fels.life

Have you tried EVERYTHING?

Ask yourself this question each time you feel down, and listen to the motivating and uplifting song "Try Everything " by Shakira. This song pushes you to get back up even though you may repeatedly fail. Originally from the 2016 Disney hit movie Zootopia, this tune inspires people of all ages never to stop or quit.

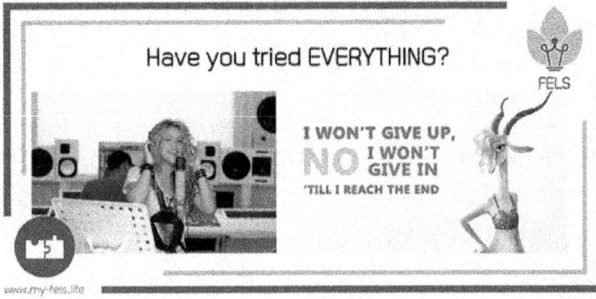

Have you tried EVERYTHING?

I WON'T GIVE UP, NO I WON'T GIVE IN 'TILL I REACH THE END

What's Your Fuel?

Do you think you or anyone else should be eating these foods?

We all know that excess sugars and carbs can pollute your body and mess with your moods & cravings.

What's Your Fuel?

Post such shaming pictures and use the hashtag *#NotMyFuel* to proclaim that they are not the right fuel for your body. Instead, use # MyFuel for delicious, healthy foods!

Gene Editing Technology (CRISPR)

Some of us may have seen the recent Netflix documentary Unnatural Selection, which delves into the high-tech world of genetic alteration. Indeed, the discovery of gene editing techniques using CRISPR-Cas in the 1990s was a landmark human achievement. CRISPR-Cas is a natural defense mechanism inherent to bacteria that splice invading DNA. Bioengineers harnessed it to " edit out" and target unwanted genes in people, which has obvious potential uses in disease prevention. Aspiring biotech entrepreneurs may have good opportunities here.

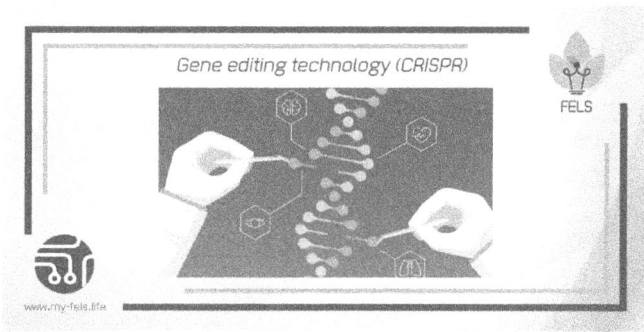

Gene editing technology (CRISPR)

FELS

www.my-fels.life

Inkyz

Luna

FELS

Who listens to trap?

www.my-fels.life

Who Listens to Trap?

Romanian music producer Inkyz has given a new flavor to the Trap genre by fusing various Eastern and Western tunes with melodies that sound like unintelligible lyrics—the results are mystical!

Check out one of their best songs: soundcloud.com/inkyz/anymus.

Book Recommendation: The Start-Up J Curve, by Howard Lowe

This profound book confirms what most savvy entrepreneurs should already know—that startups take a big dip before they start to rise. Filled with practical tips and steps for success, it can help most founders and investors be patient and resilient through the low times and wait for the highs to come.

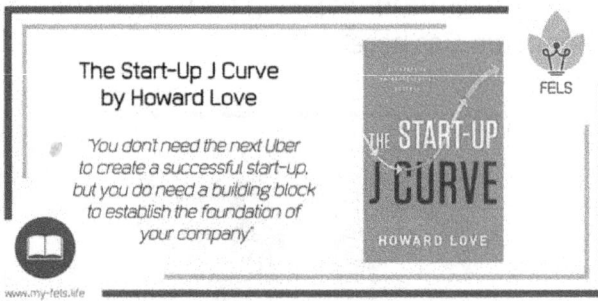

The Start-Up J Curve
by Howard Love

"You don't need the next Uber to create a successful start-up, but you do need a building block to establish the foundation of your company"

THE START-UP J CURVE

HOWARD LOVE

FELS

www.my-fels.life

Indoor Sky-Diving

This safer alternative to real extreme sport can be useful for those who fear dropping out of a flying plane or for those who want to get a taste of the feeling before they go for the big one.

iFly is a popular provider of this activity and has various locations around the world.

FELS

Indoor Sky-Diving

www.my-fels.life

Healthy or not? Keto Ice Cream

Popular creamery chain Kind Kones presents some healthier alternatives to ice cream, including sugar-free and Keto varieties sweetened with xylitol (like this tasty chocolate sorbet shown). Other flavors are also made with coconut or cashew milk rather than dairy. Give it a try!

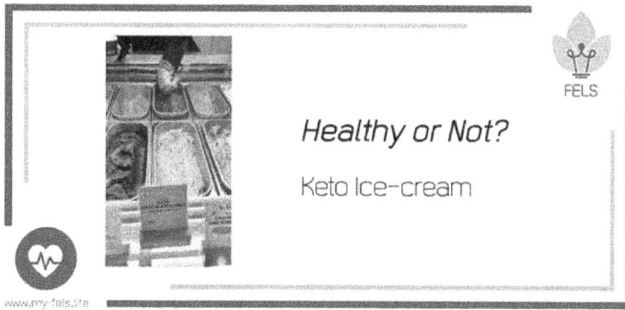

The Kuduro Dance – Dazzling 10 Years On!

Take a moment to watch this catchy song again. Nearly 10 years ago, it brought a dance and Zumba craze to the world and inspired several Portuguese, Spanish, and English remixes. The song features Lucenzo and Big Ali and was beautifully shot on the old streets of Havana, Cuba. (www.youtube.com/watch?v=f9aMmSzIHnl)

Sprawling Jakarta: Fast-Rising Center for Business & Tech

Jakarta, Indonesia, has been exploding with urban sprawl and modern architecture. More recently, a new super airport terminal and paid transit system have given the city the infrastructure boost it needs to become a regional hub for advanced business and technology. With its attractive 265-million-person market, Indonesia boasts many successful startups with unicorn potential and a goal of continued growth.

About Antioxidants

Antioxidants are useful in small amounts as they help clean up our cells and potentially help them survive longer (i.e., extending our lifespan or delaying signs of aging). Good sources for these are green tea and berries, though there is no need to overconsume them.

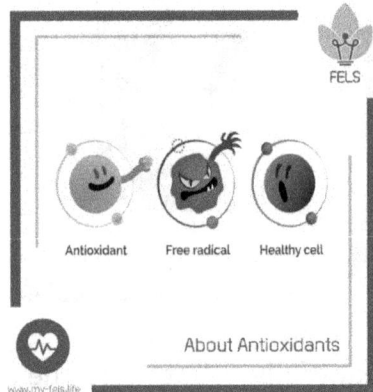

Healthy or Not? Chinese Crispy Duck

Duck is generally healthy, even with its fat, though it is much better roasted rather than fried. Just go easy on the sauce (which tends to be super-sweet) and the floury pancakes on the side.

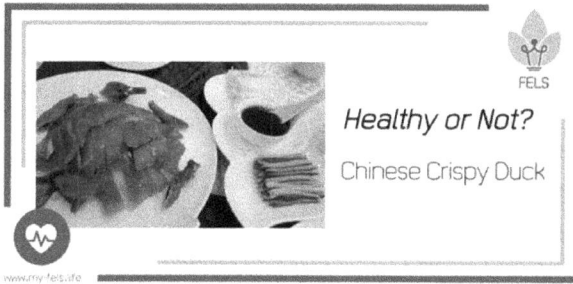

Healthy or Not?
Chinese Crispy Duck

Flying a Small Plane

This thrilling activity can help you improve focus and develop a heightened awareness with fast reactions.

Find an airfield near you that offers options for taking command of a small aircraft with a trained pilot alongside you; explore the skies!

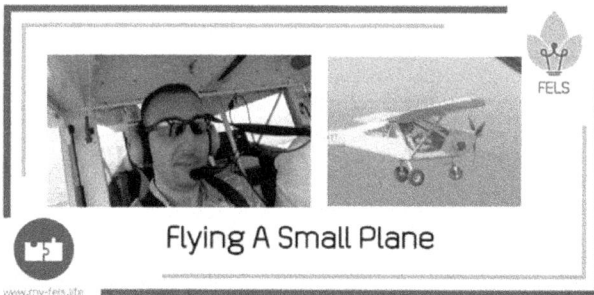

Flying A Small Plane

Old Athens City: Cradle of Greek Civilization

This amazing archaeological site once housed the capital of ancient Greece, which had renowned literary and philosophical centers.

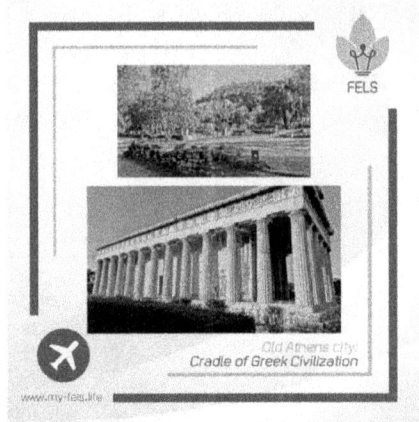

Old Athens city:
Cradle of Greek Civilization

Ancient Greece also developed many mathematical and physical concepts that we still use today.

Good place to visit and reflect on how early sciences and knowledge came about!

Book Recommendation: The Formula – Universal Laws of Success, by Albert-Laszlo Barabasi

In this pioneering examination of the scientific principles behind success, a leading researcher reveals surprising ways to transform achievement into success.

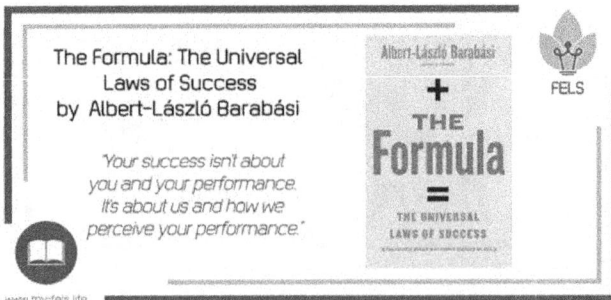

The Formula: The Universal Laws of Success by Albert-László Barabási

"Your success isn't about you and your performance. It's about us and how we perceive your performance."

Albert-László Barabási

+

THE

Formula

=

THE UNIVERSAL LAWS OF SUCCESS

CGI Cats – Creepy or Cute?

www.my-fels.life

CGI Cats – Creepy or Cute?

Computer-generated imagery has transformed the theatrical makeup and costumes of the original '80s Cats musical into their modern tech equivalents... and many people seem to dislike this. What do you think? Will CGI technology make movies and art more weird-looking and less attractive, or are they a welcome advancement?

3-D Street Art

It's always good for smart and savvy business people to cultivate their taste in art and culture, as that helps expand and balance the mind. In recent years, this art form has been popular in various parts of the world. Artists create realistic drawings that appear to have depth when seen from the right viewpoints. These amazing samples were on street display in Dubai in 2016; feel free to admire them and find similar local exhibits in your city!

3-D Street Art

www.my-fels.life

"Seeing The Code"

Most of us may remember the famous scene towards the end of the popular movie The Matrix back in 1999 when the main character Neo (played by Keanu Reeves) is finally able to see through the code of the computer matrix around him and realize the underlying mechanism behind the environment surrounding him.

"Seeing the code" can mean understanding things deeply and visualizing their inner workings.

We should all foster and practice this important life skill to see things as they are, without the shroud of false or misleading appearances.

Learn to open your mind, be sharply observant, and remember that things aren't always what they seem!

Seeing the Code

www.my-fels.life

FELS

Activity: Mountain hiking

Walking up a small mountain or rocky outcropping is a nice way to clear your mind, exercise, and catch a great view of the world below. For example, this rocky hill in Arizona is just a short climb from the roads below and offers an amazing sunset view of Phoenix.

Try trekking safely in an area near you. You'll feel your muscles working while breathing fresh mountain air!

Activity: Mountain hiking

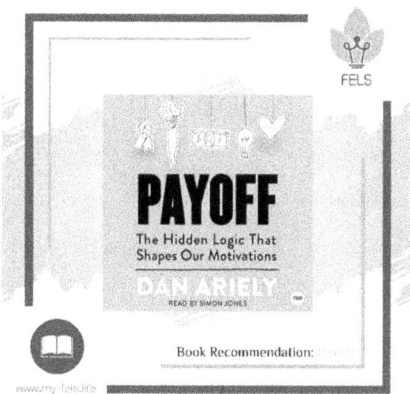

Book Recommendation: Payoff

In this landmark book, author Dan Ariely lays out the foundations of human motivation and why people tend to do what they do.

Understanding concepts like our built-in effort/reward systems and intrinsic vs. extrinsic motivation factors can help us negotiate more successfully with people and encourage them to do meaningful things in work and relationships.

About Radioactivity

Radioactivity is a curious phenomenon indeed, the fact that certain materials can break up spontaneously and release radiation of smaller particles. Discovered in the late 1890s by scientists Becquerel and Curie, it has since had numerous applications in various fields, such as medical treatment, power generation, and defense.

Some drama productions have recently been released regarding this topic, including the movie Radioactive, which highlights the life of Madame Curie (played by Rosamund Pike), and the HBO miniseries Chernobyl, which shows the nuclear catastrophe that occurred in 1986.

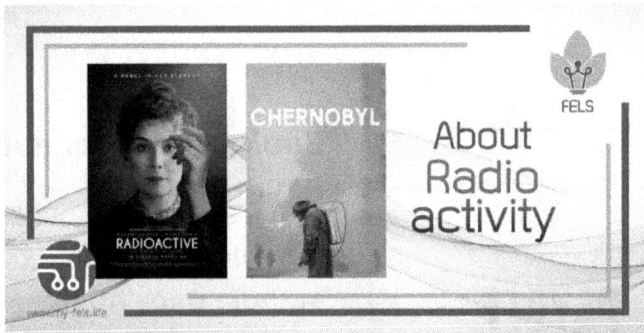

Understanding The Glycemic Index

The Glycemic Index (GI) is an important concept to grasp. It describes how much different types of carbohydrates can control the body's fat storage. Foods with a high GI, such as sugars and refined carbohydrates (e.g., white wheat products), strongly and immediately cause the body to store more fat.

Foods with a low GI, such as dark carbs and vegetables, have a minimal effect on that and thus are recommended to be eaten more often. Beware that fruits and honey have a high GI due to their sugar content and should not be consumed liberally!

Fiber Power

Dietary fiber is a useful food component that can help your body digest and remove waste more effectively and lessen the bad effects of carbs. As a component of plant cell walls, it is found only in plant products and not animal products.

Foods high in fiber include bran, whole grains, beans, nuts, vegetables, and some fruits. Get lots of fiber in your diet—around 20-30 grams are recommended daily.

Activity: Animal safari

Seeing and interacting with animals in the wild is quite an enriching experience. Because we are typically sheltered in our city homes and offices, we seldom encounter most animal types except domesticated pets or captive creatures at the zoo.

Seeing them in their natural habitat and innate behavior is very different. A safe place to do that is a safari park, where the animals are fed and comfortable.

These pictures are from a park visit in Mauritius. They feature majestic predators in their more loving and playful poses!

The World From Above

What a good time to admire how our world looks from above, naturally with its windy rivers and rugged mountains, without the polluted cities. Aerial photography can be an interesting hobby, and it's amazing what amazing views you can capture from an airplane window—if you opt for that seat!

See this specialized page on my travel blog for the full-picture collection (http://www.aimanstravelblog.com/aerial).

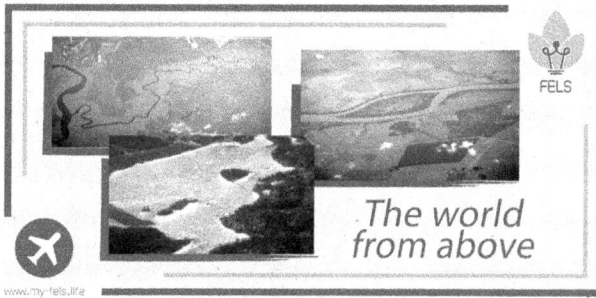

AI Revolution?

No doubt that artificial intelligence is rising fast and strong. We've all seen recent examples like the new Google bots that can communicate over the phone with natural human speech and responsiveness, advanced machine learning applications, and the like. We've seen some recent books that foresee a complete revolution coming

in this field, such as the semi-fictional novel "Origin" by Dan Brown[1] , which shows AI taking over the world, and also the business book "Life 3.0" by Max Tegmark[2] , which predicts all the various human-like functions AI will soon be able to do. What are your thoughts on where this is heading?

Go Organic or Not?

Organic foods will not necessarily make you lose weight, though they are better for long-term health.

Foods that match their natural condition and are free of chemical additives or contamination can help avoid inflammation and toxicity. In contrast, processed foods are quite harmful to us. It's always advisable to eat fresh, natural, toxin-free foods.

Though they may not help with weight loss, you will certainly feel the benefits regarding mood and concentration, sleep quality, and overall well-being.

Phages – Business Opportunities?

Phages are useful viruses that can be used to destroy harmful bacteria.

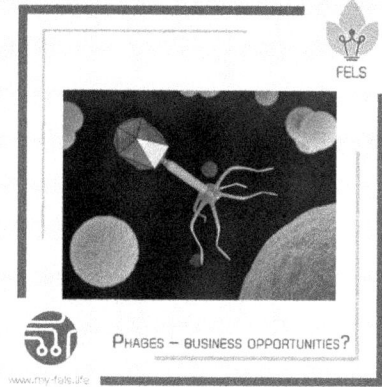

Discovered by European scientists around 100 years ago, phages' name comes from "Bacteriophage," which means bacteria-eater. Given the rising need for innovative medical solutions, phages pose a great opportunity for aspiring biotech startups to conduct advanced research in this field and develop new, potentially life-saving offerings.

A recent TED talk by Alexander Belcredi shed more light on the topic and its potential uses in fighting "superbugs," i.e., antibiotic-resistant bacteria.[3]

Have You Heard Some Chinese Pop?

Many of us have heard of K-pop and other Asian-Western fusion music, though Chinese pop tends to be lesser known outside of its own country. For example, this fancy song by popular Taiwanese singer Jolin Tsai has catchy Latin/Gypsy style tunes and lavish

Have you heard some Chinese pop?

www.my-fels.life

pirate-themed costumes and has made waves online since its release back in 2004. As entrepreneurs and ambitious people, we try to appreciate various art forms and find inspiration from the beaten path!

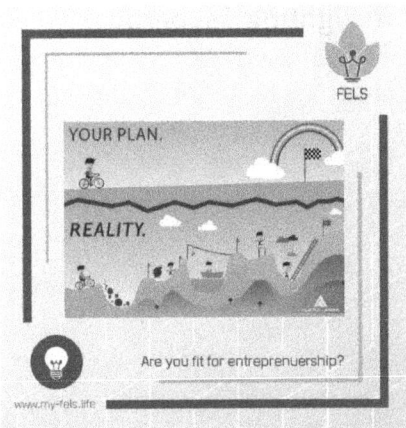

Are you fit for entreprenuership?

www.my-fels.life

Are You Fit For Entrepreneurship?

Entrepreneurship and startup culture have become buzzing fads around the world in recent years... but can anyone be an entrepreneur?

The truth is that starting up a new business is always a risky and bumpy affair, an emotional roller-coaster full of uncertainties, market adversity, and financial worries. It's a long journey with no clear end in sight, testing a person's resilience and persistence to the highest level, which may be fun for those who thrive on stress and risk but not so much for others who crave more stability and clarity. Although it can be quite rewarding, it's always advisable to think carefully and assess your situation before embarking on these pursuits. This article may help: https://rosssimmonds.com/40-signs-takes-entrepreneur/.

A Day in York

If you want to clear your mind and find new inspiration, spend a day in York, England. Its historic structures, colorful riverfront, and vibrant old-town shopping alleys offer a fresh perspective—a pleasant contrast to our daily lives in big, noisy cities. The city's compact size makes it easy to wander around on foot and take in the charm while calming your mind and preparing for your next challenges.

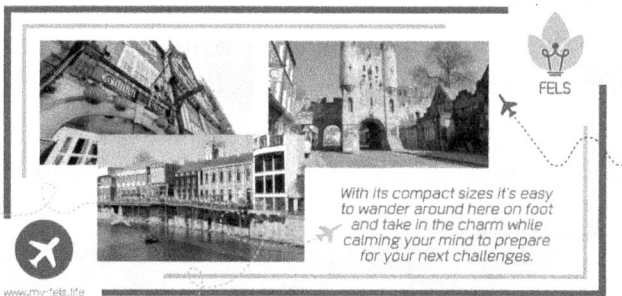

FELS

With its compact sizes it's easy to wander around here on foot and take in the charm while calming your mind to prepare for your next challenges.

www.my-fels.life

Book Recommendation: Range

In this insightful book, author David Epstein presents well-researched arguments to explain how, in our modern world, "generalists" (people with a broad range of experience) can have an advantage over specialists with a narrower field. The book shows that it sometimes takes an outsider or late starter in certain fieldwork to bring fresh perspectives, using methods and tools unfamiliar to the specialists who may be too focused on their scope to notice how things are done outside of it. It's, therefore, important for us to acquire a wider base of general knowledge and gain exposure to many fields that could spark our next insight.

Tallinn – Fusion of Old & New

The capital city of Estonia has an interesting dichotomy with a historic old town area over 1,000 years old and neighboring modern high-tech business districts.

Tallinn has preserved its charming old town close to its original condition—even with people dressed in ancient medieval clothing and restaurants serving 14th-century food—and, in recent years, has gained new fame as one of the world's top centers for technology and entrepreneurship.

La Gozadera: A Unifying Song

Released in 2015, this popular "multinational" song reached over a billion views as it touched people with heartfelt lyrics cheering for human unity and solidarity across borders and cultures (over a dozen Latin nations are mentioned by name in the lyrics).[4]

La Gozadera: a unifying song

The original video was filmed in the charming old streets of Havana, Cuba, and later remade by adding footage from similar-looking streets in Casablanca, Morocco. It is a beautiful remix with Arabic beats and lyrics, following the theme of international friendship and peace, setting aside quarrels and differences.

With its name meaning "the huge party," The song has quite a catchy rhythm and features a unique "head-spinning" dance that has captivated millions around the world!

Book Recommendation: Stay Hungry

Famous comedian Sebastian Maniscalco poured his heart into this humorous memoir about striving for success. Using profound stories of his life's ups and downs, he likens his hunger for food to his constant hunger for learning and progress. The book contains many important lessons on perseverance, focus, and never giving up despite what challenges may come. This entertaining read can remind all ambitious entrepreneurs to keep up that passionate hunger in life!

Activity: Desert Dune Bashing

Being out in nature and tackling its inherent challenges is always fun. Desert activities such as 4×4 dune-bashing, quad-biking, and similar treks are a nice way to enjoy pristine scenery while putting some skills to the test! Take a day to clear your mind with some sandy rides, surreal sunsets, and evening campfires that will inspire and remain in memory.

Activity: Desert dune bashing

Thingyan Water Festival

To mark the Burmese New Year (around mid-April), this unique festival features the throwing/spraying of water around cities and on people passing by to symbolize annual spiritual purification, "washing away" any accumulated misdeeds or bad luck. The festival is timed to mark the end of the hot/dry season in the region and also coincides with the Thai New Year celebration known as Songkran.

These photos capture the thick of the action from Yangon, Myanmar, where the ritual is most widely held, where people gather and drive around in pickup trucks to be drenched in water!

FELS

THINGYAN WATER FESTIVAL

www.my-fels.life

The Scoop on FinTech

The rising wave of startups in financial technology (known as FinTech for short) is among the fastest-growing sectors in modern business. FinTech startups are disrupting and revolutionizing various parts of the financial domain, such as digital banking, peer lending and payments, wealth management and robo-advisory, and, perhaps most famously in recent times, blockchain and cryptocurrencies.

Although startups in this field may face many regulatory barriers and societal scrutiny (typical of any "innovative" money dealings), entrepreneurs still have opportunities to create solutions that simplify the financial system while generating useful insights from big-data analytics.

The reflections and insights shared in this chapter embody the essence of the *Flourishing Entrepreneurial Lifestyle (FELS)*—a journey of growth, learning, and inspiration. These blog reflections offer a glimpse into how entrepreneurs can embrace creativity, resilience, and a sense of purpose to navigate the challenges of entrepreneurship.

I have lived the FELS life for the last 10 years as a serial entrepreneur, world traveler, nutrition enthusiast, and more. I have been involved in over a dozen technology startups as an innovator. As a digital nomad, I have visited over 95 countries. As an avid learner, I have read over 300 insightful books over the last decade. I regularly hold speaking and mentoring engagements to help entrepreneurs and other ambitious individuals grow and fulfill their potential.

This book combines amusing anecdotes from my journey with stories and valuable insights from dozens of successful people across various fields and locations who were interviewed for this purpose. The content is presented in a bite-sized format, reflecting the short blogs and social media posts where it originated, and it has a visual style designed to entertain and inspire.

By engaging with these reflections, you are invited to see how the principles of the FELS lifestyle can shape your path toward success and fulfillment, one thought, one habit, and one inspiring story at a time.

Join the movement in the language of your choice:
www.my-fels.life

About the Author

AIMAN KABLI IS A seasoned entrepreneur, mentor, and thought leader who has dedicated his career to empowering others through innovation and holistic growth. With a background in Industrial Engineering, an MBA specializing in Strategic Management, and advanced studies in Entrepreneurship and Innovation at Stanford University, Aiman blends technical expertise with a deep understanding of the entrepreneurial mindset.

Aiman's journey spans diverse roles—from holding senior positions at global organizations like *Unilever*, the *International Monetary Fund*, and *Emirates Airline* to founding and managing innovative startups such as *eleva8or.com*, a matchmaking platform for entrepreneurs and investors. Along the way, he has mentored hundreds of startups, advised accelerators and incubators, and shared his insights on global stages, including Startup Grind.

Aiman's passion for travel, continuous learning, and cultural exploration has taken him to over 95 countries, where he draws inspiration from diverse experiences. Beyond his professional pursuits, he is deeply interested in health, technology, photography, and the arts, constantly seeking new ways to innovate and grow.

Through his entrepreneurial journey and the creation of the *Flourishing Entrepreneurial Lifestyle (FELS)* framework, Aiman invites you to embrace a new way of living—one that aligns ambition with purpose and cultivates success that transcends the bottom line.

Join the movement in the language of your choice at www.my-fels.life.